T0318168

CYBER SECURITY

Cyber Security
An Introduction for
Non-Technical Managers

Jeremy Swinfen Green

Mosoco Ltd, London, UK

Routledge
Taylor & Francis Group

LONDON AND NEW YORK

First published 2015 by Gower Publishing

2 Park Square, Milton Park, Abingdon, Oxfordshire OX14 4RN
52 Vanderbilt Avenue, New York, NY 10017

Routledge is an imprint of the Taylor & Francis Group, an informa business

First issued in paperback 2020

British Library Cataloguing in Publication Data
A catalogue record for this book is available from the British Library.

The Library of Congress has cataloged the printed edition as follows:
Green, Jeremy Swinfen.
  Cyber security : an introduction for non-technical managers / by Jeremy Swinfen Green.
     pages cm
  Includes bibliographical references and index.
    ISBN 978-1-4724-6673-0 (hardback) -- ISBN 978-1-4724-6674-7 (ebook) -- ISBN 978-1-4724-6675-4 (epub) 1. Business enterprises--Computer networks--Security measures. 2. Computer security. 3. Corporations--Security measures. 4. Computer crimes--Prevention. I. Title.
    HF5548.37.G737 2015
    658.4'78--dc23
                                                              2015010130

ISBN 13: 978-1-4724-6673-0 (hbk)
ISBN 13: 978-0-367-60611-4 (pbk)

Contents

Introduction

Cyber security involves the process that organisations need to put in place in order to address cyber risks. These are the risks to organisations (and ordinary people) caused by digital technology. These risks can cause damage to:

- organisational assets including money;

- operational efficiency;

- organisational reputation.

They include the theft of money from online bank accounts, the theft of personal data for fraud purposes, deletion of data or compromise of computing machinery resulting in damage to business efficiency, damage to an organisation's reputation caused by hijacking of social media accounts, the loss of strategic IP such as a new design due to the loss of a mobile device, or a failure to spot counterfeit goods being sold online.

Cyber security is accepted as a major issue around the world; for instance Britain and HM Government is supporting a number of initiatives in the area while the UK and the USA have close cooperation in this area. However, it is often thought to be the domain of specialist IT professionals. It is important to understand that cyber security needs to be managed across organisations and not just within the IT department. Unfortunately, many managers outside IT feel they are ill equipped to deal with cyber security and the use of jargon makes the subject hard to understand. For this reason cyber threats are worse than they really need to be.

The reality is that non-technical managers need to understand and manage cyber security. This is partly because there is a need to be able to question the competence of IT managers (they are not omniscient, as the way that the NSA let Edward Snowden gather and leak confidential information shows). It is also because many of the risks stem from people (careless, ignorant or malicious people) and badly designed processes (often processes which are so cumbersome to use that people find ways of working around them) rather than from technology. For instance the big data breaches at Target in 2013 and JP Morgan in 2014 came as a result of employees falling for 'phishing' scams rather than clever hackers finding a way into corporate networks through sophisticated programming.

This book is not a 'how to do' book. Instead it tries to explain cyber security and the nature of cyber threats, including technical ones that tend to be scary because they are full of jargon (such as SQL injection, DDoS attacks and zero day threats) in a way that board directors and non-technical managers, such as accountants, should be able to appreciate. The intention is not to turn people into cyber specialists able to counteract hacking attacks. Rather it is to enable senior managers to oversee the efforts of IT professionals in this area and, equally importantly, to ensure that organisational functions beyond the IT department are cyber secure.

PART I
Introducing Cyber Security

(1) Cyber Security and Cyber Risk

Economic prosperity, national security, and our individual liberties depend on our commitment to securing cyberspace and maintaining a secure and reliable Internet. Our critical infrastructure continues to be at risk from threats in cyberspace, and our economy is harmed by the theft of our intellectual property.

US President Barack Obama

DEFINING CYBER SECURITY

Cyber security involves the steps organisations need to take in order to address the risks they face from their use, and their employees' use, of digital technology, especially IT networks, the Internet and mobile devices.

Cyber refers to 'computers'. You could just as well talk about 'digital security' in that modern computers are driven by 'digital' technology. However, 'cyber security' is the term adopted by UK government and is in fact (at least according to Google Trends) a slightly more popular term than 'digital security'.

Some people prefer to talk about 'information security' as being clearer and less like jargon but I would argue that information security is not the same as cyber security: rather it intersects with cyber security, because not all information is digital and not all digital risk or cyber risk is about information.

Cyber security is a major issue for organisations worldwide. According to the Center for Strategic and International Studies, total global losses from cybercrime are probably at least $400 billion a year. Cyber crime losses at UK retailers totalled £505 million in 2013 alone.

And that's just cybercrime. There are many other major sources of danger from cyber technology such as wasted investments, the increased power of customers, reputational damage, the accidental sharing of strategic information, and the huge increase in compliance failures around data protection and other regulations.

Cyber risks can be caused by many things. They can involve a hacker, perhaps a criminal or a political activist, penetrating an IT network to steal data.[1] But they will just as often involve the accidental leakage of secret information or personal data caused by a careless or naive employee, the theft of information caused by a disaffected employee (or an employee

---

1   In this book 'data' and 'information' are largely used interchangeably. They are of course different, although cyber risks apply to both of these terms in fairly similar ways. Definitions of data and information (as well as of knowledge and wisdom) are given in the glossary at the end of this book.

who is planning to join another organisation), or reputational damage caused by unhappy members of the public using social media.

And the result can be major damage. This damage can be direct financial loss through theft or fines, reduced sales, operational disruption, increased recruitment, credit or supplier costs, a loss of competitive advantage or reputational damage.

Despite the use of the jargon word 'cyber', it is important to understand that cyber security is not just about managing the risk to computer networks from hackers or from equipment failure. These are important risks, generally managed by the IT department or an outsourced supplier. But risks that cyber security processes need to manage extend far beyond this and can be found across organisations. They might include:

- Leaving a laptop computer that holds an unencrypted file containing a list of customers' personal data on a train.

- Posting strategically important information on a public website or a computer service that is not adequately password-protected.

- A failure to spot and act against a website selling counterfeit copies of the handbags you produce.

- The teenage son of the CEO using the CEO's iPad to access the company's Twitter account and posting some 'amusing' tweets.

- The Marketing Director losing her personal smartphone which automatically connects to her office email account, allowing people to read sensitive emails.

Generally many of these sorts of incidents will be outside the IT department's area of responsibility, which is why they need to be understood by the board and management generally.

This isn't to say that IT security shouldn't be at the centre of any cyber risk management process. Of course it should. But the risk management process needs to go way beyond IT system security.

Case Study: HMRC and the Lost Disks

According to telecom network EE, nearly 10 million mobile devices were lost or stolen in 2013. There have been numerous examples of work devices containing personal or sensitive information being lost. Sometimes these devices are relatively large – laptops or smartphones, but often they are small USB drives which can easily be mislaid.

Back in 2007, two computer disks were sent by unrecorded internal mail from HMRC in Washington, Tyne and Wear to the National Audit Office. The disks never arrived.

The disks contained records of around 25 million people in the UK and were in fact a complete record of the government's Child Benefit database. Data lost included names, addresses and dates of birth of children, together with the National Insurance numbers and bank details of their parents.

The disks were password-protected, but the encryption used was weak and could easily have been broken.

While the carelessness of a junior official was blamed, it has been suggested that cost cutting might have made things worse. The NAO had asked for bank details to be erased from the database prior to them being sent but HMRC had refused on the grounds of cost which had variously been reported as £650 and £5,000.

The data loss has been linked to the abandonment of plans for a national ID system as it strongly fuelled the argument that data in such a system would not be secure.

Search 'HMRC NAO lost disks' for a number of sites covering this story.

CYBER SECURITY IS GROWING IN IMPORTANCE

Cyber security is constantly growing in importance. Why is this?

- More and more organisations are operating online and so becoming more reliant on the Internet.

- More devices are connecting to the Internet (not just computers and smartphones but security cameras, air conditioning systems, even motor cars) increasing the opportunities for systems to be disrupted or information to leak out.

- More people are bringing powerful personal computers, in the form of smartphones, to their workplaces and using them to access work information.

- Companies are increasing the amount of data they create, capture and store online.

- Computer programmers including hackers and criminals are getting more sophisticated and building on previous cybercrime tools.

- More and more 'DIY' cybercrime tools are being offered online, for prices as low as $50.

But there is no need to panic. While it is inevitable that some damage will be caused to most organisations by internal and external people behaving maliciously or carelessly when using digital technology, there is a good deal that can be done to reduce the likelihood and impact of these cyber risks.

WHERE DO CYBER RISKS OCCUR WITHIN ORGANISATIONS?

As mentioned earlier, cyber security needs to address risks across the whole of organisations and not just within IT departments. This is why board directors and managers across organisations need to understand them. Here are a few examples:

- *HR managers* need to understand how social media misuse, such as bullying or spying on employees, can lead to discrimination or unfair dismissal cases.

- *Sales managers* need to understand that exchanges with clients on Facebook or Twitter can have contractual implications.

- *Factory managers* need to understand that failing to change the default passwords of machinery that is connected to the Internet may leave them open to the risk of damage to operational efficiency.

- *Marketing managers* need to understand the risks of divulging personal data about customers online, for instance in social media platforms.

- *Designers* need to understand the risk of storing 'in the cloud' confidential information about products and services that are under development.

- *Sales managers* need to understand the risks of storing confidential data on laptops that use public wi-fi when they are out on sales calls.

- *HR managers* need to understand the risks associated with libel from allowing colleagues to post pictures and comments about office parties and other events they attend in an official capacity.

- *Finance managers* need to understand how easy it is to publish restricted financial information accidentally.

- *Compliance managers* need to understand the risks of employing agents who communicate with consumers via social media in a hard-to-regulate way.

- *All managers* need to understand the risks that phishing scams and 'malvertising' (malicious advertising) can bring to their business.

- *All managers* need to understand the risks of losing personal computers (including tablets, smartphones and

USB sticks) that contain corporate data because they have been used at work.

- *All managers* need to understand the risks of disposing of digital devices that have been used to access and store confidential corporate information.

In addition all managers have a duty of care to their employees. And digital technology can put employees at personal risk:

- Are your employees at risk of being mugged violently because they are carrying expensive digital equipment in public?

- Are you exposing the property of your employees to the risk of theft by asking them to post information about an overseas conference they are attending?

- Are you exposing your employees to increased risk of identity theft by asking them to post certain information online such as their birthday?

- Are you putting your employees at risk of being accidentally exposed to inappropriate material (pornography, violence) for instance by clicking on a fraudulent email link?

- Are you causing your employees to feel stressed by asking them to deal with public messages during an online social media crisis?

- Are you failing to prevent your more unpleasant colleagues from bullying other employees on social media?

- Are you exposing colleagues who have access to valuable data on digital systems to the threat of blackmail?

The UK's Health and Safety Executive includes information on health and safety issues associated with cyber security on its website. It states that:

> *Accidental failure or malicious attack on process control systems could result in loss of system-critical safety functions such as interlocking and emergency shutdown systems and disruption of control of the process, potentially resulting in serious risks to operators and possibly the public.*

And finally, because cybercrime, data protection and other regulations, hacktivism (politically motivated hacking), and industrial espionage are strategically, and sometimes even existentially, important, board directors and non-technical managers need to be able to quiz and confront IT managers about the effectiveness of the job they are doing.

Duty of Care and the Otomewo Case Study

An example of the risk that employers fail in their duty of care is shown in the 2013 case Otomewo vs Carphone Warehouse which found that employers can be liable for the actions of their employees on social media even if they are on private social media accounts if an incident happens 'in the course of their employment'.

In this case two of Mr Otomewo's staff in a Carphone Warehouse shop took a mobile phone without permission and used it to update his Facebook status with words that he found deeply upsetting. In effect the judgment found that the company had failed to take reasonable steps to prevent this harassment and was therefore liable.

A clear social media policy outlining potential disciplinary actions might have helped with their defence.

I'M A STRATEGIST. I DON'T DO TECHNOLOGY

Cyber security is too important to be left to the IT department. Of course strong IT systems underpin cyber security. But there is much that managers outside IT need to be aware of, even if they don't have any real understanding of technology. In particular all employees need to be educated about 'cyber-safe' behaviour; and business processes need to be designed that don't open organisations up to unnecessary cyber risk.

An effective cyber security strategy needs to address three things:

● technology;

● business processes; and

● people.

Non-technical managers cannot be expected to be experts in IT technology. However, they should feel comfortable with the basic principles, at least insofar as they extend to cyber security. Happily, these principles are less complicated than you might think.

Non-technical managers can, however, be expected to understand processes and people. And processes and people are just as important as technology in ensuring cyber security.

For instance, lax security processes can have nothing to do with cyber technology. Consider the case of the hard drives containing confidential patient data that were stolen from an NHS hospital in Brighton in 2010. A thousand hard drives that were due to be destroyed were stored in a locked room in the hospital, supervised by NHS staff. However, at least 250 went missing and some ended up for sale on eBay. The supervision and room security process that allowed this to happen was nothing to do with a lack of knowledge of IT – although perhaps a dismissive attitude to the importance of technology may have been behind it.

Similarly back in 2007, US soldiers' ignorance of social media caused the destruction of several US Army helicopters. The soldiers had posted photographs of the helicopters on social media, unaware that photographs posted on social media often contain information referring to the location of the person posting the photograph. Iraqi insurgents used this information to locate and destroy the helicopters. This failure owed nothing to technology systems; it was a simple failure to foresee a risk and educate people about avoiding it.

Even if you don't work in the IT department, there is no reason for you to think that you know nothing of digital technology. The truth is that you probably deal with digital technology every day – music, photographs, email, word-processing, smartphones, memory sticks. Accountants have to deal with accounting software, marketers have to deal with digital CRM systems, and designers have long been familiar with CAD/CAM.

There is nothing so very different about the technology used by IT departments, apart from the jargon used and the functions it performs. Company directors and non-technical manager don't really need to know how IT and cyber security systems work. They just need to know what jobs they are supposed to do (and whether they are doing them). After all, you don't need to understand how a TV works to enjoy watching it.

DIRECTORS AND CYBER RISK

The boards of many organisations are ill prepared to deal with cyber risk. According to a 2014 Ponemon Institute report (sponsored by HP) *The Importance of Senior Executive Involvement in Breach Response*, more than 70 per cent of executives say their organisations do not understand fully the risks associated with data breaches.

This lack of knowledge seems to be affecting the way that IT professionals deal with cyber security. According to the same report, fewer than half of top executives, including board members, are kept informed about the breach response process, while 65 per cent of IT practitioners said that they would modify, filter or water-down reports about a security incident.

If board members lack knowledge and lack information how can they possibly ensure cyber security and oversee the management of cyber risks? And yet it can be argued that boards have a legal responsibility to oversee risk as part of their duty exercise 'reasonable care, skill and diligence'. Certainly in the UK they have a duty to report on it.

Most boards will have at least one member with a responsibility for risk generally. In order to start a discussion about cyber risk that person (or the chairman) should ask the following questions of the board:

- Who is responsible for cyber risk oversight on the board? What information do they receive from management?

- Have we considered our appetite for cyber risk? Have we communicated this to relevant managers? As a result are we investing sufficiently in tools, preparation and training?

- Do we have an effective cyber risk management process? How often is it reviewed? Does organisational culture support our risk management processes?

- How are we monitoring risk? Would we know if inappropriate risks were being taken?

- Do we understand the legal and regulatory environment as it applies to cyber risk, including governance, data, privacy, fair trading, industry regulations and discrimination?

- How will risk mitigation enable and promote organisational strength and growth? Are we sufficiently agile in this area?

- Are our business strategies and cyber risk management strategies aligned?

If the answer to any (or all) of these questions is 'We don't know' then I hope this book will help.

Case Study: JP Morgan Loses Records for 76 Million Households

In the late summer of 2014 US bank JP Morgan Chase was subject to a cyber attack and as a result lost data including names, addresses, phone numbers and email addresses for 76 million households and 7 million small businesses who logged in online or through mobile devices.

Customers' online bank accounts were not put at risk, the bank has claimed. But even so, because of the nature of the data stolen, the bank's customers might face the risk of:

- phishing and pharming emails that mimic the bank's official messages and direct users to malicious websites to obtain login credentials;

- direct mail that fools customers by offering a reward in an effort to extract more personal information;

- phone calls from criminals pretending to be bank officials.

The attack appears to have been caused by malware (malicious code) that was inserted into the bank's network. This seems to have happened when an employee's home computer was infected and then used by the employee to access into the bank's network from home via a 'virtual private network' (VPN).

The attack appears to have continued for a month before being discovered, according to reports. And this despite the enormous sums ($250 million annually) the bank spends on security annually.

Search 'jpmorgan hacked 2014' for more information on this story.

② A Holistic Approach to Cyber Security

Organisations need adequate cyber security because of the risks posed by malicious hackers including international criminal gangs. But they are not the only major source of cyber risk. So are employees, ex-employees, contractors, suppliers and even the general public.

Understanding where cyber risks arise and who can be responsible for them is essential if these risks are to be managed effectively. A holistic approach is needed here. Yes of course you will need to look at the organisation's IT infrastructure. But you will also need to look at how your employees interact with that infrastructure. And you will need to examine how anyone else has (or could have) access to your organisation's information systems – suppliers such as cleaners and parts manufacturers, partner organisations such as marketing agencies and accountancy firms, and people including ex-employees and customers.

In other words, cyber security processes need to deal with three types of people: outsiders, insiders and a set of people that we will call 'inside-outers'.

WHO CAUSES SECURITY BREACHES?

OUTSIDERS

Outsiders are people who don't work for your organisation. These can be:

- Hackers who enjoy the challenge of breaking into your computer systems.

- Hacktivists who try to damage your organisations because they disagree with what it does.

- Criminals who are trying to steal information from you in order to sell it, or who perhaps are threatening you in an attempt to extract protection money.

- Unscrupulous competitors (or foreign governments) who are conducting industrial espionage.

These people can do several things to achieve their ends. They can download software ('malware') that destroys your computer systems, perhaps by corrupting data or making your computers stop working. They can sneak in and steal your money, information or data. They can even start publishing false information on assets like your website or Twitter page which can cause reputational damage.

Case Study: TV5 Monde Hacked by Islamic State Supporters

It is important to realise that hacking isn't always the result of criminals trying to steal money. Political activists are also in the habit of hacking into the prominent organisations. For instance in early April 2015, hackers who said they were supporters of Islamic State knocked out the channels of French public television station TV5Monde as well as posting material on its social media feeds to protest against French military action in Iraq. The damage to the broadcaster was substantial. At the time the network's director-general Yves Bigot, was quoted as saying 'Our websites and social media sites are no longer under our control. We can only broadcast pre-recorded programmes'.

INSIDERS

Insiders are people who work for your organisation. Most insiders cause damage through carelessness, or perhaps simple naivety caused by the failure of your organisation to educate them about cyber risks. Perhaps they post information on LinkedIn that turns out to be of value to a competitor. Perhaps they lose their laptop and thus give strangers access to the confidential documents they are working on. Or perhaps they are fooled into sharing their username and password with a malicious outsider. The trusting nature of many people is one of the biggest cyber threats there is.

Not all 'inside jobs' are caused by carelessness or naivety. Sometimes employees are simply malicious and want to damage their employer or give a colleague a hard time. Perhaps they think they are about to be sacked (or they are planning to leave) so they steal data that might help them get a job with a competitor, slipping it out of the organisation on memory sticks, personal emails or private data stores such as Dropbox or Google Docs. Or perhaps (rather more unusual) they plant a 'logic bomb' in your network that will delete files or send out messages should their employment be terminated.

Case Study: Edward Snowden and the NSA

In May 2013 Edward Snowden, an IT contractor for the NSA, leaked the details of extensive Internet and phone surveillance by American intelligence.

Snowden leaked masses of classified documents. It wasn't hard. It is perhaps irrelevant that he was a contractor. What is relevant is that he was a systems administrator and thus had access to virtually all the files held by the NSA. As an administrator he could access any part of the network posing as another user or simply invisibly. Unlike most users he was also allowed to download files onto storage devices such as USB sticks.

Quis custodiet ipsos custodes? How could Snowden have been prevented, and how could you prevent something similar happening at your organisation?

Interestingly, as a result of the leak, it has been claimed that the Kremlin reverted to using typewriters to stop this type of cyber risk!

Another problem is the need to manage non-corporate networks. Cyber security tends to focus on the corporate network. But there may be networks other than your corporate network that have information about your organisation.

For instance employees may, with or without permission, be using public services such as Dropbox to store corporate data. The risks here may be obvious in some cases – employees storing prospect lists outside the corporate network is an obvious risk.

Sometimes the risks may not be apparent. For instance some companies have created public Twitter lists of their prospects and clients – opening themselves up to the risk of those clients being stolen. There may be links to e-commerce sites on a corporate Facebook page that provide a hint to competitors about that company's intentions. A corporate website will obviously contain information and this may be non-compliant with industry regulations or other regulations such as fair trading and data protection. A cyber security process needs to examine anywhere that corporate information (i.e. information about or owned by an organisation) can appear.

There is additionally a need to have robust processes to deal with ex-employees. Do they still have access to some or all of your organisation's computer systems? This could be information they have on personal devices. It could be (and often is) access to your organisation's social media accounts because no one has changed the password since they left. It could even be access to information held in the cloud or on third-party websites like Dropbox, again because no one has thought to deny them access.

INSIDE-OUTERS

Inside-outers are people who don't work for your organisation but who have some connection with it. They could be people such as the employees of suppliers or partner companies who have some access to your networks.

It is really important to make sure your cyber security strategy considers all 'inside-outers'. (If you discover that it doesn't then you most certainly won't be alone.) Do your auditors have access to your IT systems? And how about your marketing agencies, or some of your more important suppliers? Of course you trust the people you deal with on a day to day basis. But how carefully do they manage access to your systems?

- Who has access to your systems? Just the people you deal with on a day to day basis or all their colleagues including temporary assistants, and interns?

- Are your passwords ever shared by your trusted partner with their colleagues, perhaps when the person you normally work with goes on holiday?

- What sort of security precautions do your partner organisations take when recruiting new staff who might have access to your information systems? Is their employee training and communication around data protection and cyber risk management adequate?

- Are their technical cyber risk management processes adequate? Do they have robust cyber risk management policies and procedures?

- How physically secure are their offices?

- How much data are you allowing your partners to access and is this appropriate? For instance do you share complete customer data files (including bank details) with a printer when all that is needed is to share names and addresses?

- Do your partner organisations allow their employees to access your systems via home computers or mobile devices? If so how do they ensure these devices are secure?

- Have they had any previous instances of data loss of cyber damage? If so how did they respond?

- Are they insured against cyber risk, and if they are would this give you any protection?

One of the biggest cybercrime incidents was the 2013 data breach at US retailer Target when the credit card details of over 100 million people were stolen reportedly as a result of one of Target's suppliers falling for an email 'phishing scam'.

Case Study: Hackers Target 'Target' via a Supplier

Target is a large US retailer that suffered a major data breach in 2013 in which the personal details of up to 110 million customers were stolen. It appears that one of Target's suppliers, a heating and air conditioning company, had access to Target's computer systems. One of the employees of the central heating company had been spammed with a phishing email which resulted in their login details to Target's network being stolen.

According to reports, the criminals who had stolen the login data were then able to install software on Target's computer network designed to capture the credit card details of store customers. Target had security systems that should have detected the installation of this software but for some reason it appears that they failed to act when the malicious software was installed on their systems. This may well have been because the cyber security systems of large companies often signal many 'false positives' and as a result real dangers can be ignored.

By allowing the heating company to connect to its computer networks, Target made itself more vulnerable to attack. A chain is as strong as its weakest link and in this case the heating company was a weak link.

Was Target a weak link as well? Why did the information network that the heating company had access to connect with Target's payment system? The Payment Card Industry Data Security Standards (PCI-DSS) mandates that a company must segregate payment card data from other parts of its corporate networks. Target was compliant with this and had been audited. So what happened? If Target were compliant then perhaps it is the 10-year old PCI-DSS Standard itself that is at fault.

Wherever the fault lies (if indeed it does lie anywhere) Verizon's 2014 PCI Compliance report showed that only 11 per cent of businesses were fully compliant in 2013. This is a major issue for any organisation that handles consumer payment card information.

Search 'target hack 2013' for stories about this.

If you allow third parties to have access to your IT systems and information you will need to be confident that it is appropriate to do so. Some third parties may have their own independently audited certification and you may feel this is sufficient. Alternatively, depending on your appetite for risk, you may feel the necessity for further investigation through telephone interviews, questionnaires, documentation that describes processes, or even site visits.

Where third parties have no independent security certification you may also want to conduct your own auditing by asking a series of Due Diligence questions such as 'Who is responsible for cyber security?', 'How is information protected within your organisation?', 'How is your cyber security policy shared with employees?', and 'How is the policy kept up to date?'.

In each case you will probably want your contracts with third parties to reflect their duties to maintain confidentiality and cyber security.

In addition to an auditing process you should also consider how you will ensure that third parties comply with their claimed security processes. This may include spot visits, in depth investigations of projects selected at random, exploration of incidents that nearly resulted in cyber incidents, and interviews about how they plan to deal with emerging threats. And remember that a basic part of maintaining appropriate levels of security with third parties such as suppliers is communication. You will need to be happy that they will share any incidents or cyber security worries with you so that you can together take remedial action.

Case Study: Transcom and the Need for Good Communication

As well as being confident your business partners are secure, it is important to have effective communication with them.

The US Army logistics service US Transportation Command (Transcom) is an excellent example of how communication can break down and how that can cause a major security risk.

The US Army contracts much of its logistics services out to private contractors who are responsible for transporting US military personnel and equipment around the world. According to a Senate Armed Services Committee report, Transcom contractors were hacked at least 20 times in a single year. The report claimed that Transcom was 'largely unaware' of computer compromises arising in China that affected military contractors that were 'key to the mobilisation and deployment of military forces'. The issue here seems to be a simple one of inadequate reporting requirements imposed by Transcom on its contractors.

PHYSICAL SECURITY

Cyber security isn't just about managing remote digital threats. Sometimes hackers need to get in physical contact with your equipment to do their damage. And if they can walk into your office unquestioned they can potentially plant software or hardware that can create gateways or do other damage.

Make sure that staff always question people they don't recognise, especially if they are not wearing a visitor badge. Large organisations tend to have strict physical security but in smaller organisations it is often possible for someone who looks official (maybe carrying a clipboard or wearing a white coat) to walk around a building unchallenged. (At my university, two burly men in brown coats strolled into the common room, switched off the TV and took it out saying that it needed servicing. That was the last we saw of it.)

MOTIVES FOR BREACHING SECURITY

It is also important to understand that, whoever causes the problem, cyber security breaches can occur because people have a variety of motivations:

- *Gain*: Many cyber risks involve people outside (and sometimes inside) organisations attacking cyber systems with the aim of making money, either directly (stealing money or assets they can sell) or indirectly (using an organisation's network assets as a way of stealing from third parties such as clients or consumers.

- *Malice* or revenge: Sometimes hacktivists and other people who are angry with an organisation (e.g. disaffected employees) will cause trouble for personal reasons.

- *Mischief*: On occasion trouble will be caused by people, often young people, simply experimenting to see how far they can push systems defences or causing trouble for fun.

- *Carelessness*: Employees and other people with access to a network may cause difficulties by a failure to comply with agreed security protocols; for instance a failure to use secure mobile devices or secure passwords.

- *Ignorance*: Sometimes problems can be caused by people who are simply unaware that they are engaging in risky behaviour, for instance 'joking' with colleagues online.

Depending on the likely motivation, managers may want to prepare for and react to different damaging events in different ways. For instance attacks for gain are often going to involve the police, attacks based on malice may involve some form of negotiation, attacks based on mischief could involve an organisation trying to engage positively with the trouble makers, carelessness may result in some form of disciplinary action, while ignorance should be addressed through education.

③ The Scope of Cyber Security

One way of categorising cyber security breaches is consider how they arise. There are three main reasons:

- weak or outdated technology;

- inadequate processes;

- people who may be malicious, uneducated or naïve.

Technology-based breaches are those associated with software and hardware such as the failure of firewalls to keep out intruders, the uploading of malicious code to databases via an organisation's website, or a lack of adequate defence against 'Distributed Denial of Service' attacks designed to break your website.

Process-based breaches are those associated with weak business processes such as insufficient access control, weak password protocols, or a failure to require mobile device encryption and remote locking.

People-based breaches are risks associated with people's lack of knowledge or a motivation such as a failure to understand the potentially contractual nature of email or the use of private cloud accounts as a convenient way of bypass tiresome security protocols.

Don't think that technology, processes and people all represent totally different types of breach though. Very often a breach is caused by a combination of weak technology, inadequate processes and badly trained people.

WEAK TECHNOLOGY

Mention cyber security to people and most people will think you are talking about technology. And of course technology is fundamental to the management of cyber risk. A failure to update firewall or Internet browser software, a reluctance to invest in appropriate content and access management systems, badly coded websites, insufficient resource to sign up to threat-management or penetration-testing services: all these can increase the risk of damage to an organisation.

Finding the right (affordable, appropriate, cost-effective) technological approach to cyber security is obviously of foremost importance. Organisations need to be confident that they have the right technology in place as well as people who are sufficiently skilled to implement it appropriately.

Technology and network security is discussed in more detail in Chapter 4.

CYBER SECURITY AND THE INTERNET

Almost all organisations have some form of connection to the Internet. And that connection comes with a whole world of risk. Most of these risks are covered separately in this book but as they are so important it is handy to have a list of them in one place.

The main risks the Internet introduces into organisations are:

- Malware: computer viruses, keylogging software and other malicious code can be spread through email attachments which unsuspecting victims open; the result can be slow computers, deleted data, or hackers who gain access to corporate information networks. While corporate IT systems should protect against most malware it is much harder to protect against an employee whose home computer becomes infected with keylogging software and who then logs on to the corporate network from home.

- Malicious websites: websites that host malicious code that can infect the visitor's computer; people are often tricked into visiting these websites via phishing scams or fraudulent adverts.

- SQL injection: Badly coded websites can allow criminals to download code into databases simply by typing computer code into online forms (such as login forms); the databases are then instructed to divulge secret information such as customer details.

- Cross-site scripting: A badly coded corporate website can enable criminals to infect the computers of visitors to that website, potentially creating reputational damage and a loss of trust.

- Unapproved activities: employees access high bandwidth sites to download movies or watch streamed content, clogging up corporate networks and making Internet access slower for everyone else.

- Copyright infringement and piracy: employees using corporate equipment access copyright material such as movies illegally or use copyright illustrations in presentations and other public assets.

- Social media: employees spend large amounts of time on social media sites, reducing their operating efficiency.

- Social media marketing: enthusiastic but badly informed marketing executives waste money by chasing after meaningless campaign goals or damage the organisation's reputation with inappropriate or badly managed campaigns.

- Information leakage: employees download strategically significant information to servers outside the organisation's control, for convenience or personal gain, creating a potential data leakage risk.

- Computer infection: individual work computers become infected with viruses and used as 'zombie' computers, controlled remotely to undertake felonious activities; an organisation that fails to take enough care to ensure computers are clean could potentially be vicariously liable for these illegal activities.

- Denial of Service: hacktivists and other malicious people damage an organisation by bringing down its website and thus its ability to trade online.

- Risks from the 'Internet of Things': increasingly equipment that would not be thought of as a computer – security cameras, industrial machines, lighting systems, etc. – are connected to the Internet and these can act as an insecure gateway for hackers trying to penetrate a corporate network.

Non-technical managers should be aware of all of these threats and able to ask IT managers how they are all managed.

A FAILURE OF PROCESS

Cyber security breaches are frequently caused by a failure of process – or a failure of people to follow agreed process, generally because they don't see that it is important or because the process makes their life more difficult in some way.

True, there are occasions where no process within an organisation can guard against a breach: a disaffected senior IT manager; an unknown bug in a commonly used software system; a determined hacker backed by the resources of a foreign government.

But much of the time security risks can be identified and mitigated by tightening up internal business processes. These processes will sometimes be the responsibility of the IT department – implementation and maintenance of adequate firewalls around an organisation's computer network for instance.

Often the risk management processes will be (or at least should be) the responsibility of another function – the way the marketing department contracts with an outside agency perhaps, or the rules people operate under when using social media at work.

Take the processes around securing internal IT systems. There are a number of approaches that can be taken. Which approaches are used will depend on both the appetite for risk an organisation has and the resources available to it:

● The most important data (strategically important data and personal data about customers and employees) should be stored as encrypted files. It is possible to enforce encryption policies automatically through the use of a document's content to trigger encryption in appropriate cases, although of course systems to do this cost money so whether or not you implement them will depend on your appetite for risk as well as your available resources. Otherwise education about the importance of encryption, e.g. of HR managers with responsibility for employee data, may well deliver an appropriate level of risk management.

● In the most sensitive of cases, consider whether encryption details should be hidden from people who have access to encrypted files. The 'four-eye principle', where one administrator manages user access to the content and another manages encryption and decryption, ensures that neither administrator alone has the ability to steal information; some commentators feel that this approach would have stopped Edward Snowden being able to share so much sensitive information from the US National Security Agency in 2013.

- File access requests can be logged automatically to point up suspicious behaviour and to provide an audit trail; for instance if an employee demands access to large numbers of files this might warrant some form of investigation.

- 'Two-factor authentication' should be implemented when people access certain accounts; this involves two 'factors' such as a password and a one-off code that is sent to a mobile phone being required for login; this type of security is increasingly available of social media accounts and should be implemented when possible and especially when devices like laptops and smartphones that are capable of being taken out of a secure office environment are being used (note that insisting on this can be thought of as a nuisance and so appropriate education, backed up with monitoring and sanctions, may be necessary).

- Appropriate security software can prevent unauthorised copying of documents; however, this may be impractical (or too expensive) for many organisations and it may be more practical simply to encrypt a few of the most sensitive files using standard tools available within document creation software (such as Word and Excel).

PEOPLE: THE MAIN RISK?

Ask an IT professional where the main risks to their IT systems lie and they are unlikely to say 'hackers'. Instead they will probably point to their colleagues (outside the IT department of course).

And in fact employees present a huge problem for cyber security for a number of reasons. For instance:

- They are trusting and leave themselves open to fraud such as the theft of log on details.

- They are busy and stressed and will try to avoid any security processes that slow them down, especially if they don't understand the reason for them.

- They are naïve and often have no idea that doing certain things (such as sharing passwords or clicking on links in emails) can result in security problems.

- They are career minded and may avoid security processes if it helps them collect information that might be useful to future employment – information which if it leaked could cause their current employer difficulties.

Managing people requires a combination of documented guidelines and policies (so that people know what they should do), training (so they understand what the guidelines and policies mean in practice), monitoring (so that managers can review the extent that guidelines and policies are being adhered to), and disciplinary processes (so that people understand the sanctions that will apply if they fail to follow guidelines and policies).

DIFFERENT TYPES OF DAMAGE

In order to take cyber security seriously it helps to understand the type of damage that can arise from cyber technology.

You might think that the damage is limited to the sort of information theft that Sony Pictures suffered from in late 2014 when sensitive emails were published. Or perhaps the damage that Playstation suffered at the same time when the Lizard Squad Gang[1] attacked its online network.

Case Study: Sony Pictures

In late 2014 confidential information owned by Sony Pictures was released by hackers. The data included personal information about employees, emails between employees about actors, and copies of unreleased films. In addition Sony Pictures social media accounts were hacked. And data on corporate computers was wiped. The attackers called themselves 'Guardians of Peace' and one of the demands they made was the cancellation of a film about the North Korean leader Kim Jong-un. Some people have blamed the North Korean government for the hack but this is by no means certain.

There are a number of cyber security learnings from the Sony hack which include:

• Encrypt all sensitive data. Many of the documents containing personal and corporate information were not encrypted in any way.

• Do not store passwords in the same place as password-protected documents. Although some files were password-protected, there are reports that many were accompanied by a folder containing the passwords.

• Use two-factor authentication. Although it is not known how the attackers accessed the Sony data, it is likely they used stolen or credentials provided by insiders, which would have been useless, had the company used two-factor authentication.

---

1   Ironically the Lizard Squad were themselves hacked in early 2015 and the names and bank details of people who had paid money for their DDoS attack services (which had been stored in a totally unencrypted form) were published online.

• Keep sensitive personal data separate from other data. According to leaked information, folders for salary, heath and other personal data were stored in the same directories as other data.

• Carry out regular external security checks, to ensure obvious security risks are eliminated; and to check that, if attackers are able to get into the network, it is difficult for them to move around without restriction.

These types of attack involving data theft and the disruption of computers are common. But the damage from a cyber incident can take many forms ranging from the ransacking of bank accounts to reduced employee motivation. Examples of damage include (in no particular order):

• Theft of money. Money stolen by criminals accessing company bank accounts has been estimated to be worth £1.3 billion pa according to a 2011 report prepared by Detica for the UK Cabinet Office.

• Being 'locked out' of computer systems often as a prelude to a ransom being demanded. In the past ransom-ware attacks have mainly been aimed at individual computer users in small businesses and at home rather than corporate networks; however, there is evidence that large organisations are increasingly being attacked in this way and in late 2014 an Australian TV station was temporarily forced off air as a result of a ransom-ware attack.

• Damage to computers that drive information systems or manufacturing processes. Malicious software can cause damage to computer systems, such as the deletion of files or the disruption of data processing resulting in a loss of business efficiency. An example of malware disrupting a system is the Stuxnet "worm" that seriously damaged Iran's nuclear centrifuges in 2010.

- Identity theft for the purposes of damaging reputation or selling counterfeit goods. Identity theft on social media is often simply mischievous, for instance when someone hijacks a prominent organisation's social media account. An example of this is when the British Labour Party apparently promised 'free owls for everyone' as a new campaign pledge. However, identity theft on the wider Internet is a serious problem.

- The loss of personal data (especially employees' or customers') that can lead to fines for compliance failure. European Union rules now mandate a fine of up to 5 per cent of global turnover (or 100 million Euros) for personal data loss by organisations controlling personal data for more than 5,000 people. Loss of personal data (e.g. customer details such as names and addresses) can happen because a computer becomes infected with malware. But it can (and frequently does) also happen because of human carelessness: for instance leaving a laptop on a train or sending a computer file to the wrong person via email.

- Reduced efficiency of working practices and business processes. For instance efficient collaboration on a project could be affected by an attack on a corporate network.

- An inability to accept or process online sales. Typically this is caused by 'Denial of Service' (DoS) attacks which send a lot of traffic to websites causing them to crash or function very slowly, resulting in lost sales. An innocent Denial of Service effect was seen when Michael Jackson died in 2009 and websites like Google and Twitter slowed perceptibly due to the amount of traffic they had to handle. The average time it takes an organisation to handle a DoS attack is a little under an hour and with an average cost per minute of downtime estimated by cyber security company Incapsula as averaging $40,000 it is easy to see that these attacks can be very damaging to companies reliant on e-commerce.

- The leakage of strategic information such as design blueprints or the details of intended acquisitions. Strategic information can also be lost because of malware or carelessness. The theft of strategic information and IP is big business costing UK businesses £7 billion a year according to the UK Cabinet Office.

- The loss of IP protection of designs and trademarks as a result of previously protected assets being published inappropriately.

- Lowered staff morale and related difficulties in attracting top talent. Damage (or a failure to prevent damage) to the physical and mental well-being of employees, customers and other third parties can cause morale problems. For instance employees could suffer from stress as a result of dealing with angry members of the public during a social media crisis or a service failure.

- Legal suits for cyber bullying or discrimination. These actions happen relatively frequently with companies being found 'vicariously' liable for the inappropriate actions of their employees.

- Accidentally entering into unfavourable contracts or accidentally varying existing contracts. Cases of this happening through unwise emails have been recorded. It is likely that similar cases will happen (or have already happened) as a result of social media use.

In addition, consequential damage as a result of a cyber incident can include:

- Reputational damage that can affect an organisation's credibility with suppliers, financial markets, banks, and customers.

- The cost of 'clearing up' any damage caused and preventing it from happening in the future. This can be more expensive than the initial incident.

Case Study: Intesa Sanpaolo Bank Hoax

Cyber incidents can have a major effect on share price. On 25 April 2015 the shares of the Italian bank *Intesa Sanpaolo* dropped suddenly by 4 per cent. Hoax emails had been sent to journalists saying that the CEO Carlo Messina had resigned after manipulating earnings to the tune of €2 billion. It wasn't true. But the emails linked to a website that looked similar to Intesa's and an email address for the press team that was very similar to the real one: stampa@intesasanpaolo-group.com rather than stampa@intesasanpaolo.com. The press team were quickly on the case and corrected the story. But not before some traders had lost money and no doubt others, perhaps including the perpetrators of the hoax, had made money.

It's important to realise that the damage isn't always what it may appear to be at first. For instance, in June 2015 it was reported that hackers had (again) broken into the computer network of the US government's Office of Personnel Management, compromising the personnel records of 4 million federal employees.

Data including staff social security numbers were stolen. This could result in identity theft and a good deal of personal inconvenience to staff. In fact the US Government offered victims insurance against identity theft in the wake of the attack.

However, the real significance of the breach is the fact that the data could be used for attacks on other US government systems by enabling effective spear-phishing. US government employees, receiving highly credible emails containing personal data 'from' their employer, might believe that the emails are trustworthy, click on links in them, and be steered to sites where keylogging software could be installed or where requests were made for log in information. These techniques could then be used to gain access to sensitive US government information or systems.

All of this sounds quite frightening. But the reality is that few organisations have ever faced an 'existential' crisis because of breaches in their cyber security. And in any case, while it is true that the threat from cyber risks is constantly growing, there are plenty of processes that can be put in place to manage them as will be shown in the second part of this book.

PART II
The Main Threats to Cyber Security

(4) Systems Risks

The 'traditional' approach to cyber security, and one that most senior managers will be aware of, involves the protection of corporate information within a corporate network. IT managers are seen as people who guard against intruders by using complicated 'firewalls' and anti-virus software. It's important but, like the process of cleaning the director's washrooms, we don't really need (or want) to know how it is done.

Well, that may be true in so far as it goes. But it really doesn't go far enough. There is a need for directors and senior managers to take an interest in the actions of IT staff. As well as being motivating for them, it's vital that IT managers should have their assumptions questioned and their decisions explored. Appropriate questioning may uncover resource issues or knowledge gaps that need filling. IT is after all a rapidly moving field and without appropriate and continual professional development IT managers cannot hope to keep up to date.

WHAT DO IT SYSTEMS REALLY DO?

Simply put, IT systems need to make data and information easily accessible to authorised users while at the same time preventing unauthorised people from accessing or modifying it. In other words IT systems need to ensure that an organisation's information is:

- accessible when required and in a format that is easy to use;

- accessible only by authorised people;

- able to be altered only by authorised people.

It is not generally the role of the IT manager to decide who is 'authorised', which is one reason why the active involvement of non-IT managers in corporate information systems is essential.

IT systems need to be able to protect information when it is in one of three states:

- Information 'at rest': Information at rest is being stored somewhere ready for someone to access it. Information and data in this state is generally protected by network security designed to prevent someone crossing a 'boundary' into the place where it is stored. Increasingly though it is recognised that boundaries are permeable and so information and data (at least the most sensitive) also needs to be protected by encryption. In addition it is all too possible that information is at rest outside the corporate network for instance on a third-party email system. Do you know where all your sensitive corporate information is stored?

- Information 'in transit': Information in transit is being sent from one computer to another, for instance as a file transfer between a corporate network and a mobile device, as an email between two people, or as a file downloaded onto a USB and then uploaded to another computer. Sometimes information in transit can be protected by the method of transit (such as web based 'SSL' data transfers) but at other times it is extremely vulnerable if it hasn't been encrypted.

• Information 'in use': Information in use is being read or manipulated. Where the context of use, such as an organisational network, is secure the data may be secure. But where the context of use, such as a personally owned smartphone, is insecure because it is outside the organisation's IT system, then the information may well be at risk.

'ALWAYS ON' INFORMATION

Almost every organisation needs constant access to its information. And that means having IT systems that are always on. What can go wrong with IT systems to prevent this? Consider two possible (I hope unlikely) scenarios:

1. The computers in your office become inaccessible, perhaps because of an electricity cut, perhaps because you can't get into your office due to flooding.

2. The information on all the computers in your office is erased by malicious software that has been inserted in a virus attack.

How would your organisation continue to operate without access to all your data and information?

When you put these two scenarios to your IT team, there are two types of information to consider: your email; and all the files and folders that underpin the various functions of your organisation.

Email is generally 'mission critical': most organisations would find it very hard to operate without it. Therefore it is important to ensure that your email system is working and that you can access it even if you cannot access your office. In fact your email system is relatively easy to manage and may well already be handled by servers (computers) that are off site or 'in the cloud' so that anyone with the appropriate passwords can access their work emails from anywhere, even if your office is beneath two metres of water.

The files and folders may be harder to manage, especially if your organisation holds a large amount of data like video. You may accept a bit of a risk by holding the information on computers in your office and backing all the files up once a week onto drives that are held off site (a pretty common strategy for small and medium businesses). If something happens to your computers you can 'rebuild' them using your backup files. You may have lost a few days of data and it may take you a few days to get access to your files, but it isn't a total disaster (especially if your email service is still working).

Alternatively you can choose to hold all your files off site or 'in the cloud' so it is easy to access from anywhere, whatever the state of your office. This is often a good solution although it can be expensive to hold *all* of your data in this way if you have a lot of data to store and back up (lots of video for instance). Companies with this problem will generally prioritise the data they have, storing recent data off site and backing up older data (and larger files) in cheaper physical storage that is harder to access.

If you are holding data off site then it is important to be confident that it is as secure as it would be locked up in your own office. If you are using a reputable supplier then it probably is rather more secure than it would be in your office. Loss of data because your supplier fails is some way is a risk, however, and you do need to be aware of it.

Companies providing data storage services will (should) offer data backup as an integral part of what they do (in case their computers become inoperable for some reason). Note though that relying on the same company to store your data and back it up does expose you to extra risk and in some circumstances it may be appropriate to employ separate backup facilities.

REDUCING THE CHANCE OF TECHNOLOGICAL BREACHES

There isn't much you can do about your office flooding (apart from relocating off the flood plain) but it is possible to guard against most of the technology-driven threats to your information security. These threats include:

- Network hacking attacks where intruders try to get into your computer network in order to steal information or place malicious code. You need to be confident that you have adequate intrusion detection and a strong firewall.

- Website attacks where if you have a poorly coded interactive websites (i.e. a website where visitors can type information such as login details into forms on the site) people can gain access to your database (in an SQL injection attack) or infect the computers of your visitors (in a cross-site scripting or XSS attack); the solution to these attacks is high-quality coding.

- Attacks that use your website domain name including 'Denial of Service' attacks designed to overload the computer that hosts your website and 'Pharming' attacks designed to take your visitors to a malicious website instead of to your own website; various technical strategies exist for defeating or reducing the impact of these attacks.

- Social engineering attacks including 'Phishing' attacks where people are fooled into giving details such as login names and passwords when they receive a credible but malicious email; the solution here is principally education although there are services that will alert you to known 'signatures' (e.g. typical wording) or sources (e.g. websites) of scams.

Notice I called this section '*Reducing* the chance of technological breaches'. That's because there is no possibility of eliminating the threat of a breach entirely. Hackers are generally ahead of the game, with security professionally running to catch up. In addition the trusting nature of most people also opens IT systems up to cyber risks. All you can hope to do is to reduce the chance of a cyber attack being successful and, if it is successful, of reducing its effect.

NETWORK HACKING ATTACKS

Even if you don't know much about computer technology you are probably very familiar with the idea of hacking. The aim of a hacker is generally to insert some nasty code on your corporate network in order to achieve something such as stealing data or breaking a system.

Hackers generally target networks in one of two ways. They may target individuals who they think have access to a network and try to steal their login details, or fool them into giving them over. Or they may attack the network directly, looking for weak passwords, unprotected connections, badly coded websites, or flaws in the software being used by the organisation under attack.

Typically there will be four stages to a direct attack on a network:

1. Arriving, where the intruder is looking for vulnerabilities and ways in. They may use techniques such as phishing, pharming (see below), malvertising (see below) or 'war dialling' which involves telephoning all the numbers owned by a company in the hope of finding a number used by an unprotected Internet connection. Large companies may employ cyber security intelligence services in the hope of identifying when they come under attack; however these services are expensive and not possible for everyone.

2. Breaking in, the actual penetration of the network by the intruder.

3. Concealing, the phase where the intruder secretly copies data, destroys it or leaves malicious code behind, perhaps designed to give them remote control of your system, undertake certain actions such as copying and exporting files in the future, leave a 'back door' open for future penetration, or lie dormant until a certain date or event.

4. Disappearing, where the intruder coverers their tracks, sometimes destroying huge amounts of data in an attempt to do so, and leaves.

Sometimes the intruder may know of a bug in the software you are using that no one is aware of. This can be commonly used software like a web browser or a computer operating system. Because no one knows about the bug the intruder can get in easily. This is known as a 'zero day' or 'zero hour' attack as the software developer has had zero time to create a 'patch' (a solution to the bug).

Networks can be protected against hacking in a number of ways, with:

• a firewall between your organisation's network and the outside world including the Internet that will prevent illegal in-coming (and if necessary out-going) traffic;

• a port scanner to see what ports (doorways from your network to the outside world e.g. the Internet) on your network are open and how well they are defended;

• an intrusion detector to identify if someone tries to access your network illegally; this is important, especially for large and prominent organisations, as illegal access attempts may herald an attempt at a crime;

• a virus checker to identify and quarantine any viruses that arrive in email messages, on USB sticks or via websites; your security system should also be checking that there is no spyware (that could monitor keystrokes and record passwords) on your network.

Network protection is often about protecting the 'doorways' into a network from hackers. The feeling is that if the walls are strong enough we will be safe. But what happens if they are not? You should ask 'what would happen if someone does penetrate our network defences, however unlikely that may be?'

Case Study: The Carbanak Banking Attack and Phishing

In February 2015 reports started to circulate about the Carbanak banking attack. This was described as an "advanced persistent threat" attack although the techniques used were not particularly advanced (the attack was "persistent" though in that is lasted many weeks).

Security firm Kapersky Labs reported up to $1 billion had been compromised and possibly stolen in a phishing attack that enabled Carbanak "back door" malware to be downloaded to the IT networks of up to 100 financial institutions. This malware enabled malicious people to enter the IT networks of those institutions at will. Once in to a network, the criminals looked for likely IT admins and recorded screen activity to enable them to manipulate the network.

They were able to steal money in a number of ways: by setting up fake accounts and having associates collect money from them, by forcing ATMs to disgorge cash, again collected by associates; and by using ebanking to transfer funds to the criminals' existing bank accounts.

ATTACKING WEAK WEBSITE CODE

If your website is badly coded then it provides opportunities for malicious people to attack you. There are two main ways of attacking you through the code of your website: SQL injection and cross-site scripting. Both of these techniques are very common.

SQL injection is a technique that allows hackers to use weak website coding to 'inject' SQL commands (SQL is a computer language used to control databases) into a form on a website, such as a login form, to gain access to the data held within your database. Instead of typing in login details, computer code is typed in instead and submitted. The SQL code tells your database to do something like destroy all its contents or email the data to the hacker.

Case Study: SQL Injection Attack on US Retailer 7-Eleven

SQL injection has been around for many years, since the late 1990s. Perhaps the biggest example of how it has been used by criminals occurred in 2009 when Albert Gonzalez and two Russian co-conspirators hacked into the payment systems of a number of retailers, including the 7-Eleven chain.

Gonzalez was charged with stealing data relating to 130 million credit and debit cards and is alleged to have been responsible for the largest SQL injection attack so far.

SQL injection attacks are not complex. The solution is a purely technical one: ensuring that database software is up to date and appropriate database coding is in place.

SQL attacks don't just present a risk of stolen credit card details though. 'Ordinary' emails can present a risk if they are stolen. In January 2015 the Banque Centrale de Genève (BCGE) was held to ransom. Hackers, using an SQL injection technique, penetrated one of the bank's websites. The site, which was used for customer service, held emails from customers who had problems with, and questions about, their bank accounts. The hackers stole over 30,000 of these emails.

The Rex Mundi hacking group initially asked for $30,000 not to leak the stolen emails. Later the demand was dropped to $12,000. However, the emails were made public, and BCGE claimed they had refused to pay the ransom. BCGE downplayed the incident. No bank details had been compromised: these were simply emails to and from bank customers and bank officials.

But was there really a significant risk? Certainly there was reputational damage to BCGE: people expect bank security to be a lot tighter than this. And there may have been real damage to some overseas clients who were using the bank as a tax shelter: as Rex Mundi tweeted 'We would like to wish a merry tax audit to all the non-Swiss account holders listed in the BCGE files'. More important is the risk to ordinary account holders who will now be at risk from criminals using the information in the emails to create credible scam phone calls and emails.

The damage from these attacks doesn't stop with the consumer whose details are compromised. The organisation that is hacked may suffer loss too. In 2010, the brokerage firm Davidson and Co. was fined $375,000 by the USA's Financial Industry Regulatory Authority (FINRA) after suffering an SQL injection attack. According to FINRA, 'Broker-dealers must be especially vigilant about protecting their customers' confidential information, which includes ensuring that their technology is sufficient'. The firm had failed in this duty.

Cross-site scripting (XSS) is a technique that allows the hacker to inject malicious code into your website. Any web page which allows a visitor to enter information which is then passed to a database can be vulnerable: login forms, address fields, etc. Your website doesn't appear to be altered but once the code has been injected then subsequent visitors to the website can be attacked.

Vulnerability to both SQL injection and XSS is generally caused by poor coding practice. It may be useful to ask IT specialists how confident they are in the rigour of the code used.

ATTACKS THAT STOP YOUR WEBSITE WORKING

'Denial of Service' (DoS) attacks are very common and are designed to stop your website from working. These attacks target your Domain Name Server (DNS). Domain Name Servers are computers that act as the telephone directories of the Internet. A DNS will translate a domain name like www. mosoco.co.uk into a string of numbers that can tell computers where to find the information stored in the Mosoco website.

Denial of Service (DoS) attacks involve a felonious computer operator sending lots of traffic to the computer your website is stored on, in the hope of overwhelming it. A Distributed Denial of Service (DDoS) is much the same thing except that a network of remotely controlled 'zombie' computers (a 'botnet' or network of robot computers) is used to attack you (zombie computers are generally owned by innocent people who probably have no idea that their computer is being used to attack someone else). A bit more jargon: application layer DDoS (or layer 7 DDoS) attacks target a specific function in the user interface (e.g. search, email, e-commerce) as opposed to the whole of your website's infrastructure. They require less resource and are easier to disguise as ordinary web traffic.

The basic strategy for surviving a DoS attack is to have (or hire) more bandwidth than your attacker, so that the increased traffic doesn't overwhelm your connection to the Internet. This isn't always possible, however. Large companies that run their own domain name computers may need to employ specialist DDoS mitigation or threat intelligence services if they are reliant in any way on their website. Smaller companies that use an external ISP service to host their website should ensure they have discussed their options for defending against DDoS attacks with their ISP providers if they are reliant on their website.

ATTACKS THAT HIJACK YOUR WEBSITE VISITORS

Another way of attacking you via your website is to hijack visitors who want to go to your website and take them somewhere else where they can be taken advantage of.

Cache poisoning (also known as Redirecting) is a method of fooling DNS servers into sending visitors who want to visit your website to a malicious website instead. This website probably looks like your site but is designed either to upload malicious software into your unfortunate visitor's computer, or to fool them into giving important information such as the login details to your site.

Registrar hijacking involves an attack on the Domain Name Servers you have your domain name registered with. If they are attacked successfully then your domain name can be stolen and linked to a malicious site. Large companies may well have their own DNS servers and need to make sure for instance that relevant software is kept up to date. Smaller companies may use a third-party domain name registrar. Registering a domain name isn't particularly expensive so it is worth making sure that the company your organisation uses takes security seriously, even if they are a little more expensive. You may be able to bolster security by ensuring your website administrators need to use two-factor authentication or are only able to log in to the DNS system from particular computers (i.e. computers that use particular IP addresses).

DO YOU NEED TO BE INVOLVED?

DNS attacks are fairly technical and it isn't appropriate for a non-specialist to have charge of preventing them. This is something for your IT department or your IT supplier.

However, you should be able to ask questions about how well protected your organisation is from these attacks. One important question to ask is whether your website administrators have had specific training in protecting against DNS attacks. Especially if you are running an e-commerce operation, then you need to make sure they are up to speed on protecting against these threats.

In addition larger companies and companies that consider themselves at risk should consider investing in specialist computers and services to protect their Domain Name Servers.

Case Study: Denial of Service Attack on Spamhaus

In the spring of 2013, the Internet was slowed down by a massive Denial of Service attack by Cyberbunker, a Dutch website hosting company, on Spamhaus, a non-profit organisation that helps users filter out spam and other unwanted content.

To protect its users, Spamhaus maintains a database of servers known to be used for malicious purposes. The group had protected its users from accessing content on servers belonging to Cyberbunker, which will host content on almost anything except for child pornography and terrorism.

The attackers used a Distributed Denial of Service (DDoS) attack, which inundates the target with large amounts of traffic in an attempt to render it unreachable. In this case, Spamhaus's Domain Name System (DNS) servers were targeted. Without DNS servers websites effectively become invisible as they cannot be located.

The attacks peaked at 300 Gbps (gigabits per second), a very substantial amount of traffic and one that could have taken most organisations down. Spamhaus said it was able to cope as it has highly distributed infrastructure in a number of countries.

TAKING PEOPLE TO FAKE SITES: 'PHARMING'

Pharming is another danger that managers need to be aware of. A pharming fraud involves taking users to fake sites which are designed to upload malicious code or steal login data and other information. It can happen as a result of people clicking on malicious links in emails or as a result of DNS servers being compromised (see the paragraphs on Cache Poisoning and Register Hijacking in the section above).

Pharming is particularly dangerous on sites where members of the public can post their own content. For example in September 2014 the BBC reported that an eBay listing for an iPhone contained links that diverted people to a fake version of the eBay welcome page designed to steal their login credentials.

MALICIOUS ADVERTISING: 'MALVERTISING'

Malvertising involves using advertising that contains or leads to malware in order to infect computers. In the past this type of attack was most commonly found on social media sites but more recently malvertising has been found in a wide variety of sites including mainstream publishers and online retailers.

Malvertising can be found in animated banners but is particularly dangerous in pop-up advertising because sometimes pop-ups will upload their malware program when the user clicks the 'x' to get rid of the pop-up.

Defending against malvertising can involve:

- Ensuring users have the most up-to-date browsers as these often have the ability to warn about adverts that lead to suspicious URLs.

- Educating employees not to click on advertising (why should they be doing that at work anyway?).

- Ensuring that work computers use a pop-up blocker or set web browsers to automatically block pop-ups; note that some websites use pop-ups as part of their interface so employees will need to be aware that there are occasions that they need to allow the pop-up to appear.

WHO SHOULD BE RESPONSIBLE?

Depending on the size and type of your organisation, cyber security will be handled by different people.

If you are running a small business, perhaps a one-person consultancy or a small plumbing company, the chances are that you will rely on a security package like Bullguard or Norton to make your computers secure from viruses and hackers when you access the Internet: make sure the package you choose has both an anti-virus component and a firewall component. This is ESSENTIAL: it is the basic level of security that any organisation, or indeed individual, needs. But it is important to ensure that it is up to date and that any computer than has access to information that you value is protected with this software. As well as using a security package you should also ensure that any software you run on your computer, such as Windows, Office, Explorer, Adobe and Java, is kept up to date: where possible allow automatic updating.

Larger organisations which have their own office IT networks will typically outsource their security to a third-party specialist supplier, often as part of an IT support package. This is fine – so long as the specialist supplier is competent in IT security as well as computer maintenance. Consider how this was handled when they were appointed. Is it worth re-evaluating this question?

Another third party who may have security responsibilities is the company who created your organisation's website. Are they certain that your site is proof against SQL injection or cross-site scripting attacks? And how about the company that 'hosts' your website? How would they deal with Denial of Service attacks? (Have you asked them?) If your organisation is in any way dependent on your websites, this is an important issue to address.

The largest organisations, or organisations that are heavily dependent on IT services, may well have their own extensive IT department. It is good to have in-house resource as these people are likely to be motivated to ensure security as their jobs may depend on this! But in-house teams can bring their own risks: too much power in one pair of hands, an over-reliance on people who may not be trustworthy, or possibly 'gaps' in security where the responsibility of two specialist teams meet. In any case in-house teams need to be appropriately trained, kept up to date with new techniques, and where appropriate supported by external specialists such as DoS mitigation service suppliers.

LOOKING TO THE FUTURE

Traditionally IT professionals defend network perimeters, in an attempt to keep malicious people out. However, this approach is increasingly unsustainable. Technologies that protect network perimeters and other elements of IT infrastructure have several problems:

- They are not built to protect individual applications (software programs designed to do something on a computer such as word-processing software). This is because they rely on analysing traffic and content as it goes to and from a network, rather than seeing how that content is processed within an application.

- They cannot protect data when it is in transit or being manipulated away from the IT system as they only manage the ability to get in and out of an IT system.

- They cannot protect against attacks which happen inside the perimeter of the IT system, which means they are useless if they fail to keep malicious traffic out of an IT system.

- They cannot protect perimeters if they have ceased to exist because of private mobile devices and private cloud use.

How can organisations deal with this problem? One tactic is to focus on protecting individual applications rather than IT infrastructure. So for instance Internet of Things devices that have built in security should be used in preference to devices that rely on external security.

Gartner estimates that in 2014, enterprises spent $9.1 billion on firewalls and intrusion prevention systems, and $2.4 billion for secure Internet gateways, a total of $11.5 billion. At the same time, they will have spent a twentieth of that, a little more than $500 million, on application security.

Perimeter defence should not be abandoned even though it is not totally effective in stopping attacks. However, there should be a stronger emphasis on investing in application and file security. In addition there is a need for information security teams to recruit more application security specialists, people who understand application development, the programs used to create applications, and the runtime engines and operating systems that enable computers to 'understand' these applications.

How is this relevant to your organisation? Possibly not at all if you work for a small business. In that case you will just have to wait 5 or 10 years before common programs are improved with self-defence features. However, if you work for a large organisation it may be worth asking your information security specialists whether they are paying sufficient to building self-protecting and self-testing applications.

⑤ People and Networks

Ask an IT professional about what worries them most and they probably won't answer 'hackers'. They are most likely to say that it is their colleagues outside IT who worry them most. They have technical network risks pretty well covered. But they won't be so able to control people and process risks. That's where they need you – and you need them.

HOW PEOPLE PUT INFORMATION AT RISK

Your technical network security can be as strong as you like but unless you manage the people using it then your corporate information will always be at risk.

MALICIOUS INSIDERS

A rogue employee or contractor with access to your computer network is always going to present challenges for cyber security. Think of Edward Snowden, the IT contractor who managed to steal hundreds of sensitive files from a US security network the National Security Agency. (It is particularly worrying that the NSA is the agency responsible for defending sensitive US computer systems from cyber attack.) What can you do about this sort of thing?

You might think 'nothing' but in fact there is a good deal of protection you can offer your organisation.

First of all, you can consider ensuring that sensitive documents or areas of a network drive are only accessible by certain people. Restrictions should apply to IT administrators as well as other employees. You may want to consider ways of preventing IT administrators from having access to all areas of your corporate network through the use of passwords or access privileges. In particular handle sensitive information (e.g. employee records and customer details) on a 'need to know' basis so that access to it is restricted. Ensure that sensitive documents are encrypted so that if people do manage to access them they are unable to read them.

Remember: it is likely to be counter-productive to try to restrict access to everything or to encrypt every file. Instead consider how to prioritise your information into different levels of sensitivity. Certain information might be 'critical' and stored in limited access directories with individual files encrypted. Other information might be 'confidential' and accessible only by certain people. And other information could be 'public', capable of access by anyone but allowing only certain people to have editing privileges.

Second, if you have the resources, you can put access tracking in place so that an alert is sent to an appropriate manager whenever sensitive information is accessed, copied or modified. Again you will probably want to limit this tracking to the most sensitive information to avoid overwhelming people with information about commonplace files being accessed.

These steps are particularly important if you allow people to access your organisation's computer network from mobile devices (including laptops) or from home via a 'Virtual Private Network' (VPN) that has been set up for employees over the Internet.

And just to reiterate: when doing this, remember the principle of focusing on the most sensitive data. If you encrypt every file your organisation possesses you will merely irritate everyone and reduce productivity.

MANAGING ACCESS TO THE WEB

As well as managing what information people have access to on your corporate network, and what they can do with it, you may want to manage what websites they can go to.

Uncontrolled access to websites during working hours can in some cases be a risk to productivity and one that you therefore wish to manage. Not all employers will do this but for some it is important. In addition there is the danger of people doing illegal things on your office network such as downloading pirated movies or buying counterfeit goods: these actions could leave you, as their employer, liable.

A number of software systems and network settings are available that can restrict the sites your employees can access. For instance your marketing team may need access to Facebook during the working day, but you may want the rest of your employees only to have access at lunch time and after 5pm. Some sophisticated systems offer options to restrict what functionality can be used on sites for instance allowing people to access LinkedIn group discussions but not LinkedIn jobs.

69

Alternatively you may not want to place restrictions but you may want to be able to monitor what sites people look at. This is perfectly acceptable if it is done in an appropriate way. The Information Commissioner's website gives useful guidelines here but the main rules are:

- Tell people what they are allowed to do.

- Tell people they are being monitored.

- Only use the information you gather when monitoring for the purpose it was obtained for.

- Keep the information you gather secure and don't hold it for longer than necessary.

- Take especial care when monitoring communications that could contain personal data such as email or the content of social media posts.

PROTECTING INFORMATION FROM PEOPLE

SINGLE SIGN-ON

One of the best ways of protecting corporate information is to know who is doing what. This doesn't have to involve continuous monitoring of people. Instead it can involve forcing people to leave a paper trail of where they have been.

In order to do this you need to implement a 'single sign-on' (SSO) system. With SSO, network users sign on once to a network. They are then able to access any sites and applications automatically without having to remember another password. For instance you might arrange it that when your social media manager signs on then they are able to access your corporate Twitter account but when your HR manager signs on they are able to visit Twitter but cannot access the corporate Twitter account and post content on behalf of your organisation.

As well as making it easy for users, SSO has the advantage that when people leave an organisation it is very easy to stop their access to corporate website accounts, something that can otherwise easily get forgotten.

STRENGTHENING PASSWORDS

Passwords are, obviously, an important part of cyber security. Unfortunately passwords have many flaws largely because people find secure passwords hard to remember. As a result they tend to use simple passwords like *111111* or *password*. Passwords like this are dangerous. In fact passwords should never:

- Be fewer than eight characters (surprisingly easy to break through cycling through all the options).

- Contain a string of just numbers (again easy to break even with 'brute force' if you use fewer than around 12 characters).

- Contain words or names (password breaking software uses 'dictionaries' full of the most common words, and indeed passwords).

- Numbers substituted for letters in words (like L3tm31n for Letmein or P455w0rd for Password) as hackers are wise to this.

In the future we may be able to depend on biometric security such as fingerprints, but for the moment we are stuck with passwords.

An IT professional is likely to tell you that in order to have a secure password it has to be:

- at least 12 characters long, using upper and lower-case letters and numbers (and ideally symbols), and without any whole words or names in it;

- changed every few months;

- different for each site.

Tell your colleagues that you want them to follow these rules and expect to hear a collective sigh and cries of 'That's impossible!'

It's not. If you have implemented single sign-on, the third requirement becomes redundant as you can be given automatic login to the various sites you are allowed to go to once you have signed on to the corporate network as a whole. This means that several people can have access to a single account (e.g. the corporate Twitter account) using a single password but with their visits and actions recorded.

But let's assume you don't have SSO. How can you comply with these three difficult requirements? Of course it is important to make a sensible compromise between security and convenience: you don't want to make it so hard for people that they simply write their password to the corporate network on a Post-it® Note which they stick on their PC screen. But it is in fact reasonably simple to create strong passwords that comply with the three rules. Here's how.

First, think of a phrase that means something to you, that will be easy to remember, and that can naturally contain capital letters and numbers. For example you might think of the phrase 'I love working at Widgets4Us Incorporated, Dorking!' By using the first letters of each word I can create a password Ilw@W4UI,D! (You will need to remember the 'at' sign, the comma and the exclamation mark but the addition of symbols makes your password extra secure; not all sites accept passwords with symbols so if you are accessing many sites then you may be better sticking to letters and numbers).

Next because your IT manager insists that the password is changed every month you think of a way of adding a date code to your phrase. A very simple one would be to add the last two numbers of the year at the start and numbers representing the month at the end. Now your password (for October 2014) is 14Ilw@W4UI,D!10.

And finally you want to make the password different for each website. So if you want a password for Twitter you could for example take the first and last letters of the name, use a lower-case 't' and an upper-case 'R' and put them at the end of the password. Now your password is 14Ilw@W4UI,D!10tR – a pretty random selection of 17 characters that even the strictest IT practitioner should be happy with. But to remember it for any website all you have to do is remember the phrase, your date 'code', and your site 'code'.

Of course it is always possible that a very imaginative person could deduce your system if they got hold of one of your passwords somehow. But a machine couldn't. And in any case we are not trying to create something that is absolutely unbreakable. We are trying to create something that is reasonably secure but convenient at the same time.

AVOIDING HUMAN ERROR

Humans make errors all the time. And this applies in cyber security as much as anywhere else. In fact IBM's *2014 Cyber Security Intelligence Index* claims that 95 per cent of all security incidents involve human error.

Typical errors that have caused problems include:

- forwarding the whole of an email thread to a recipient who should only see part of it;

- sending data or documents to the wrong people by accident;

- accidentally giving strategic information away online, perhaps when discussing a new technology or new market in an online forum;

- making confidential files publicly available, perhaps in a cloud computing service, or on a server that is connected to the Internet and can be visited by search engines.

One of the biggest sources of accidental data leakage is when people send sensitive emails to the wrong people by mistake. Most people will have clicked 'Reply all' when they meant to click 'Reply' or inappropriately sent a complete thread of emails including internal discussions to an external recipient. It's easily done. Larger companies may want to employ software to help manage this Otherwise, there isn't much you can do about this sort of thing except to educate people (although some email systems have a 'Retract email' function that works for a few seconds after an email is sent).

But it is also relatively common for sensitive information to be sent to the wrong people as email attachments. There are no 'golden bullets' here. Larger organisations may choose to use automated security controls that limit who certain files can be sent to. Smaller organisations may have to rely on encrypting sensitive documents, creating directory structures for projects that separate internal and external documents, or putting words in the file title that give people a clue that they shouldn't be shared with certain recipients. (For instance a response to an RFP might include a file with external costs intended for internal consumption only and this might be called WidgetsRFP_internalPlanningDocument.)

TEACHING PEOPLE TO BE DISTRUSTFUL

Another big problem for cyber security is that people are trusting by nature. Educating them to be suspicious is an essential part of cyber defence.

The main problem is 'phishing'. Phishing (and related scams 'spear-phishing' and 'whaling') involves fooling people into clicking on links in a message via social media or email (or, in the case of 'smishing' an SMS message) that takes them through to a site that either uploads malware to their computer or asks them to input security data such as usernames, passwords and credit card details, or that simply starts an online dialogue intended to defraud.

If the target of the scam is fooled into providing their corporate login details to a malicious third party then of course, until this is known, the corporate information network is wide open to outsiders who can steal or destroy information or plant software that will hamper operations.

While some computer security systems will filter out the most obvious phishing scams, they can't identify them all. Educating people to spot phishing attacks is therefore an important tactic. There is more on this in the chapter on 'Protecting people'.

INFORMATION SECURITY POLICY

Most organisations will have an Information Security policy document. Writing one should not be a 'tick box' exercise: the policy should actively contribute to the efficiency of the organisation.

The objectives of the policy should be to ensure that employees understand what they can, and cannot, do in respect of digital systems and the information and data that your organisation creates and stores.

An Information Security policy will often include things such as:

- password requirements;

- when, which and how documents should be encrypted;

- rules around the use of portable data stores like memory sticks;

- rules around acceptable email and Internet use;

- responsibilities under privacy, data protection and intellectual property laws;

- requirements around client and corporate confidentiality.

There may also be reference to a separate Bring Your Own Device policy and a Bring Your Own Cloud policy (see chapters 6 and 7).

The policy should not set out the technical standards for network firewall for instance: there will no doubt be a requirement for such a document but not here.

Rather this should be a document that can be, and is, shared with staff and which helps them understand how they should treat the information that your organisation holds. As a manager, you should be able to understand and explain the policy to the people you work with and you should feel that it is relevant to the work that you do and not just to your colleagues in IT.

Search 'Information security policy' online and you will find lots of detailed advice and templates.

(6) Cloud Computing

'Cloud computing' is an increasingly popular concept. The idea is that, instead of having your information and software on computers in your office that you own and control, you use software and store files 'in the cloud' on remote computers that are accessed via the Internet.

It makes a lot of sense for organisations to use 'the cloud' as it can save costs and increase efficiency. But the cloud also comes with its own set of risks. Understanding and managing these risks is just as important as taking advantage of the flexibility and cost savings that the cloud provides.

WHY IS CLOUD COMPUTING IMPORTANT?

In a 'traditional' IT infrastructure, software (such as word-processing and spreadsheet software) is downloaded to individual personal computers. Employees use the software for certain tasks and the resulting files are stored either on the personal computer or, more commonly in organisations larger than a handful of people, on separate computers housed in the organisation's offices.

'Cloud computing' is a term for using computer services that are provided away from an office location and accessed via the Internet. This way of working, which can free IT departments from a lot of IT administration, is becoming increasingly popular.

Cloud computing can simply involve using software that is provided on remote computers. So for instance Microsoft is encouraging people who want to use their popular Office software (Word, Excel, PowerPoint, etc.) to rent access to it in the cloud rather than buying the software on a disc and installing it on a personal computer.

Using software in the cloud isn't really an issue for cyber security (especially as Microsoft also lets you install the software on a personal computer so you can use it even when you are not connected to the Internet).

However, it is also possible to store the files you create in the cloud rather than in your office. And this is an issue, especially when people create their own unofficial 'clouds' that are not controlled by the organisation they work for. (We will explore that shortly in the section 'Bring Your Own Cloud'.)

Cloud computing is important for cyber security because it is generating a change in the way that IT professionals think about security. In the past a great deal of emphasis was put protecting the peripheries of IT networks. Computing in the cloud makes the nature of IT networks a lot fuzzier. Peripheries become harder to defend and as a result there is a need to provide security that travels with the data wherever it is.

DOES CLOUD COMPUTING INCREASE OR DECREASE RISK?

Computing in the cloud has a different and slightly lower risk profile. The amount of risk needs to be evaluated before deciding on whether to use a cloud service. But note that an in-office service also has risks: if the office becomes inaccessible for a time or the electricity supply is cut off for some reason, then data stored in the office will become inaccessible while data stored in the cloud will still be available.

In contrast a cloud service can be used by employees based anywhere: so if the workplace Internet connection fails for some reason, employees with secure access from home computers can still be effective. For this reason, cloud computing, accompanied by a list of employees who have home broadband (likely to be most these days) and who are able to work from home, can be a low risk option for organisations although risks still exist.

DISADVANTAGES OF CLOUD COMPUTING

Let's take a look at some of the areas that impact on security:

Cloud services rely on you having an Internet connection. From time to time these do become unavailable, and while the problem is generally sorted out very quickly, when a service break happens, organisations reliant on the cloud can face problems.

The use of a third-party cloud computing supplier could also increase risk as they might:

- lose Internet connectivity;

- cease trading;

- prevent you from accessing your data as a result of a trading dispute;

- suffer a technical problem resulting in data loss.

In addition they could suffer a security breach resulting in data leakage or data loss. Hacking remains a risk in the cloud, but as organisations providing these services are specialist and often very large (e.g. Microsoft and Google) they tend to be good at securing their perimeters.

Be aware that cloud computing won't protect you from problems caused by 'social engineering' (phishing, etc.) where people are fooled into disclosing login names and passwords to devious third parties. And cloud computing service providers are just as open to the threats from hackers and Denial of Service attacks as an individual organisation is: they may be better able to handle it as they tend to be large and specialist organisations, but they may also be more prominent and thus more likely to be attacked.

ADVANTAGES OF CLOUD COMPUTING

There are many advantages to using cloud computing that may well outweigh the disadvantages:

- Disaster recovery and backups: With a traditional IT infrastructure, disaster recovery may be slower than with cloud services as there is a need to manage physical resources on which data is backed up. Cloud provider will (or should) be testing their disaster recovery plans regularly while individual businesses are often neglectful of this. However, it should be noted that using the same supplier to provide cloud services and data backup services is a risk, although it may be a sensible one to take.

- Ownership and capital expenditure: The traditional infrastructure requires an organisation to buy expensive equipment. A cloud service means that the organisation in effect 'rents' the necessarily equipment, meaning that there is no need for a large amount of cash up front; the flexibility of capitalising the IT expenditure is gone, however.

INCREASING THE SECURITY OF CLOUD COMPUTING

If files are stored away from secure organisational networks then one obvious way of protecting them is to insist that individual files stored in the cloud use strong encryption so that if an unauthorised person gains access to a file the data within it is unintelligible.

This is fine in theory but can cause inconvenience in practice, especially where more than one person needs access to the files.

More normally it will be the directories in which the files are stored that will be encrypted.

OWNING THE KEYS

Most cloud computing suppliers will offer excellent security and encryption. However, it is very important for the organisation that owns the data to be in total control of the encryption keys.

If they are not they cannot guarantee compliance with data protection standards and may well be liable if the cloud computing supplier is compromised in some way.

For instance third-party cloud computing suppliers have duties to you. But they may have stronger duties to their own national governments. An example of this is the reason given by the German government for cancelling contracts with Verizon in the wake of the Edward Snowden data breach. According to the German Interior Ministry 'There are indications that Verizon is legally required to provide certain things to the NSA, and that's one of the reasons the cooperation with Verizon won't continue'.

BRING YOUR OWN CLOUD

Bring Your Own Cloud (also known as BYOC or 'Shadow IT') involves employees using public cloud computing services such as Dropbox or Google Docs to store corporate information.

This may in some cases be sanctioned by the organisation (as being cheaper to implement than using a dedicated service). But as often as not, employees use such services informally perhaps as a way of accessing work files when they are unable to connect to the organisation's network or as a way of sharing documents with corporate outsiders who are jointly working on a project.

This can cause document management, security and compliance problems: organisations may not be able to police who has access to their information or which document is the 'official' version, and in some cases the information may accidentally be made public.

In practice it is pretty hard to prevent this happening unless strict restrictions on downloading files to unofficial cloud services, personal devices and portable storage media are in place.

One very common use of cloud computing is email. Most business people will have a work email address and one or more personal email addresses. Personal email accounts such as Gmail will generally be stored securely in the cloud. But Google's security doesn't mean those accounts won't be hacked – generally because the passwords account holders use to protect them are often inadequate. For that reason using personal email accounts for business is often frowned on. But a lot of people do it anyway. In March 2015 Hilary Clinton was admonished by officials in the USA after using her own private email address for official business, contrary to State Department rules.

One way of managing this (especially for smaller organisations who don't have the resources to sign up to dedicated cloud storage services) is to set up private corporate cloud accounts, which could be as simple as a corporate Dropbox account. However, if you decide to do this, note that there is still a risk of people copying data for illicit purposes for instance as attachments on emails or on memory stocks smuggled out of the office.

Whatever the solution, you should also put in place:

- appropriate policies (e.g. when cloud services can be used, who needs to be notified when they are used, what sort of data is not allowed to be stored in unofficial cloud accounts): search for 'cloud computing policy' and you should find a number of templates;

- education about the policies and about using cloud services securely;

- appropriate security (encryption of certain sensitive files and folders);

- if appropriate and feasible, the monitoring of networks to see when files are transferred to personal cloud computing services.

Case Study: Apple iCloud

The theft of hundreds of photos, some nude, of celebrities from Apple's iCloud service in September 2014 left the celebrities, and Apple, red-faced. How could it be so easy to break into Apple accounts? The answer is that, with many people careless about their security, it only required a little patience and a small amount of information.

The Apple cloud system automatically backs up documents and images stored on people's iPhone and iPad devices. It was perhaps an obvious target for hackers, who shared the private images on a message board, from where they went viral on the Internet.

In order to access Apple accounts people needed a few things: a celeb's email address, their date of birth, and the answers to two out of three security questions. This information is often readily available – and the security questions can often be guessed or researched.

Ensuring that passwords are strong and security questions are un-guessable is a key to making systems like this safer.

BUT I LIKE USING THIS SOFTWARE ...

Another problem organisations face is employees using their own favoured software to run certain tasks. This is sometimes known as 'Bring Your Own Application' or BYOA.

BYOA, a concept similar to BYOC, involves employees using their own favourite applications to conduct work tasks. It's unlikely that they will use a different word-processing tool or spreadsheet software as these are business 'essentials'. But they may well use a favourite project-management tool or data visualisation package.

Why does this matter? For four reasons:

- The favoured application may not be the most efficient application for the job: in this case training the employee to use the standard application may result in a cost saving.

- The outputs of non-standard applications may be hard for their colleagues to read or manipulate; of course in some circumstances this can be precisely why the non-standard application is being used.

- The favoured application may be less secure that the standard application used by the organisation.

- The favoured application may be being used illegally, putting the organisation at risk of vicarious liability for copyright infringement.

In order to manage the use of BYOA, it is sensible to audit the tools that people use outside the standard set of tools. Unofficial tools need to be evaluated – there may be a perfectly good reason they are used and if appropriate adopted by the organisation.

Preventing BYOA can be hard and ultimately relies on corporate computers being audited for the presence of unauthorised software which may be time consuming and unpopular. As is so often the case, education and flexibility is often a better path than rules and sanctions. But of course this depends of your appetite for risk.

⑦ Bring Your Own Device

'Bring Your Own Device', or BYOD, involves employees using their own personal computing devices such as smartphones and tablet computers to access, manipulate and store work documents. It is now commonplace at work.

The majority of UK adults have smartphones or tablet computers. And most people who have them bring them to work, perhaps to check up on Facebook profiles, or listen to music. However, because many people will also use these portable devices to access corporate information, some of which may be very sensitive, BYOD massively increases cyber risk for organisations.

Why does this cause problems for security? Because these portable devices can easily get lost or stolen (according to the telecommunications company EE around 10 million such devices are lost in the UK every year). And if they do get lost then it is quite possible that any corporate information on them will leak. If a device is protected with a simple pin or pattern then it will be easy to break into it. And if for instance work emails are delivered automatically to the device then inappropriate people will be able to read them.

In addition these devices frequently lack basic anti-virus software and firewalls which presents a risk if they are ever used to store corporate information or log on to corporate networks. But because they are personal devices they are next to impossible for IT professionals to control.

Furthermore many people connect their personal devices to the Internet via public wi-fi without a thought. Yet public wi-fi can be risky and so protecting mobile devices with a Virtual Private Network (VPN)[1] is essential if you want to keep information on a mobile device safe. (For more on this see Chapter 9's first section 'Keeping Mobile Phones Safe'.)

It is up to managers to educate their colleagues about these risks and put protocols in place that limit risky behaviour.

WHY IS BYOD A PROBLEM?

Mobile devices bring many benefits with them including allowing employees to have constant access to work data (and thus be more productive). However they also present substantial risks in the area of data leakage especially as mobile devices often have weak security at a time that threats to mobile security is growing.

Some organisations have recognised this and have banned using mobile devices to access work data such as emails. However, the reality is that many employees want to use their

---

1   Confusing terminology alert: VPN is used in two rather different contexts. Here as a method of protecting a mobile device when connecting to the internet via public wi-fi, and elsewhere in this book as a secure way of connecting a home computer to a corporate IT network.

mobile devices and a good number will simply ignore any such bans.

Knowing this, or perhaps in simple ignorance of the risks, many other organisations adapt a laissez-faire approach to employees using their own devices at work.

Problems can be caused in several ways:

- A device containing sensitive information is lost or stolen.

- A device containing sensitive information is sold or recycled when the owner no longer wants it.

- Unauthorised people who share the device (including family members) gain access to corporate information stored on the device.

- The device is compromised by downloading an app infected with malware.

- Third parties 'listen in' to conversations and the exchange of documents when the owner uses an insecure or fraudulent public wi-fi connection.

These situations can result in a number of different risks if mobile devices are used to store and process work data.

Most significantly, the security of personal data of clients and others (for instance a name attached to an email address or telephone number) can be compromised if the device is compromised with malware, lost or used by a third party (see the section on Rooting and Jailbreaking below).

In addition, commercially sensitive information, e.g. work emails, reports, financial spreadsheets, new designs, may be leaked if it is stored on a mobile device which is then compromised, lost or recycled. Third parties can potentially compromise a mobile device so that cameras and microphones can be controlled remotely and then use this ability to create their own commercially sensitive information e.g. recordings of a meeting or layout of a facility.

You should also be aware that employees may become demotivated if colleagues use personal mobile devices to contact them outside office hours or if they are expected to use their own personal data allowance for work purposes.

SHARING DEVICES

Another risk to be aware of is the danger of employees sharing devices that contain corporate information and login details for corporate accounts with family and friends, and even with colleagues. This can be especially risky with smartphones and tablets which sometimes can't be 'divided' into separate accounts in the way that PCs and laptops can.

If there is only one account on a tablet, and if the device is set to remember login details for corporate social media accounts, it would be very easy for mischievous people with access to the device to post inappropriate content. Mobile devices should therefore never be set to remember login details.

BYOD AND DATA PROTECTION

If personal data gets leaked this can be a major problem for the employer, even if they don't own the device from which the data was leaked. This is because the 'data controller', not the device owner, is legally responsible for any breaches of the Data Protection Act. Organisations therefore need to secure their data against loss or damage caused by BYOD.

ROOTING AND JAILBREAKING

A big problem with BYOD is that mobile devices can be rendered very unsafe by their owners. Many people feel the need to customise their own devices in some way, perhaps uploading a new version of an operating system or downloading an app that isn't supported by the phone. They do this by gaining access to the operating system of the phone (a process known as *Jailbreaking* for Apple devices and *Rooting* for other devices). Even people who are not technically proficient can manage this as there are frequently high street shops offering this service.

While there can be many benefits to the user from rooting their device, the reality is that it is fairly easy, even for a technically astute person, to download something that contains malware. This malware could in turn compromise network security.

In order to combat this, some organisations put in place mobile device management (MDM) software that will block rooted phones from accessing corporate networks. Not all organisations have MDM products in place though and even if they do it is possible to disguise the fact that a device has been rooted. This is a good reason for considering if you wish to allow any mobile devices to connect to a corporate network.

If you decide you are happy to take this risk then you may want to tell your employees that attempting to connect a rooted device to the corporate network is a serious disciplinary offence.

MANAGING BYOD SECURITY

There are a number of different BYOD strategies that can be employed by an organisation:

- Do nothing: a laissez-faire attitude to mobile devices, which are becoming increasingly powerful, is fraught with danger.

- Not allowing any mobile devices to have any access to the corporate network; a high security approach but one that may well irritate employees.

- Limiting mobile devices to accessing email and calendars; this strategy limits risk while allowing people to keep in touch with important work information when away from their desks.

- Limiting the people who are allowed to connect via mobile devices to certain trusted individuals.

- Limiting the types of devices that are allowed to connect so that, say, laptops are allowed but smartphones and tablets are not.

- Limiting the devices that have access to corporate networks to devices that have been 'doctored' by IT specialists; for instance devices may only be given access once they have been inspected for rooting; in addition devices can be divided into corporate and personal 'personas' so that personal data doesn't interact with corporate data and so that corporate data can be held and tracked securely without corporate IT having access to 'private' user activities.

- Using Mobile Enterprise Management tools: this involves the potentially expensive implementation of a managed approach to BYOD that involves: Mobile Device Management (software that tracks mobiles using the corporate network and excludes certain ones such as devices that have been rooted – see page 93); Mobile Application Management (software that controls which mobile users can use particular applications on the network); and Mobile Information Management (software that allows only approved applications to access or transmit corporate data).

- Only allowing company-owned devices to have access to the corporate network; a high security approach but one that requires the organisation to invest in mobile devices; in addition employees may feel they need to carry a second, private, device which many will find irritating (see section on COPE below).

BYOD presents major risks to organisations that can be managed in different ways. The extent to which these risks are accepted will of course depend on the organisation's appetite for risk in this area. There is no one right answer.

COMPANY-OWNED, PERSONALLY ENABLED

Some organisations, accepting that people will want to use mobile devices to access work information, and realising that there are many benefits to productivity and flexibility if this is allowed, purchase mobile devices for their employees. This concept is known as COPE (Company-owned, personally enabled).

Buying the devices is obviously a cost, but it does allow corporate IT to manage the devices and reduce the risks they represent.

COPE can be cheaper to implement than a managed BYOD system as the IT department can limit which devices it has to support, unlike a BYOD policy where the number of devices that need supporting could be unlimited.

However, as well as the cost of the devices the system may fail simply because people want their own device, not a company device – which they may regard as intrusive or as being inadequate for their needs. And because carrying two devices around is a nuisance, they simply ignore the COPE device, and use only their personal device, either trying to get round any restrictions on personal devices having access, or just not using their personal device for work purposes (with a resulting loss of flexibility and productivity).

Because of this any COPE strategy needs to build in some choice about the devices offered, and ensure that COPE devices allow users credible privacy for their personal use of the devices.

PRACTICAL CONSIDERATIONS

If mobile devices are allowed at work then a number of practical issues need consideration:

- What management of the mobile devices will be required? For instance will it be mandatory to use remote wiping software? If mandatory remote wiping is required how will the employer deal with the potential that private data (such as holiday photographs) will be wiped alongside corporate data? And what sort of password protocols will be required?

- What limits will be put on mobile devices? Will they be allowed in meetings, for instance? (They could be used for surreptitious recording by hackers or disaffected employees.) What sort of information will be allowed on them? (Downloading client lists might be risky and could technically be a breach of the Data Protection regulations if the device were to be taken outside the EU.)

- How will connection to corporate networks be managed? Will the device be able to connect on office wi-fi? Home wi-fi? Public wi-fi? And how will this be policed? Does the organisation have adequate mobile device management (MDM) security in place?

- How will events such as the owner leaving the employer or the device being lost be handled?

In order to make all these issues clear to employees who are bringing their own devices to work it is sensible to write a BYOD End User Agreement that makes the employee responsible for good security and that allows the employer certain rights (such as remotely wiping the device) under certain circumstances.

BYOD USER AGREEMENT

Organisations should adopt a formal agreement with employees who want to use personal devices to access and store corporate data. This could include the following content (you should take legal advice as to the exact wording):

1. It is your responsibility to keep corporate data safe on the device.

2. You are responsible for all costs of the device even when it is being used for corporate purposes (*this stipulation may need to be relaxed with regard to phone calls made when the employee is away from home*).

3. You agree to use a strong password (*defined as you feel appropriate*) on the device and if required to encrypt the device.

4. You agree to install remote device management on the device to allow wiping of data or locking of the device and to allow data to be wiped or the device to be locked in the event of its loss.

5. You will report the loss of the device to your employer immediately.

6. Wiping the device may result in personal data (e.g. photographs) being wiped; you acknowledge this and accept that it is your responsibility to back up any personal data on the device.

7. If an investigation into data loss, fraud or similar takes place, you agree that the device may be analysed by us, your employer, and this may result in personal data held on the device being exposed.

8. The device will not be used to store (*or it might be appropriate to say 'store unencrypted'*) the following types of data: (*the employer will then list the sensitive data that may not be stored on the device e.g. customer and employee personal records*).

9. The device will not be used to send any corporate data to other devices or systems (*it may be appropriate to include this requirement as it is difficult to track data sent from one BYOD device to another*).

10. You agree to clean the device of any corporate data prior to disposal of the device (*as an alternative, it may be safer to require the employee to bring the device to the employer for data cleansing, although of course this does require the devices to be tracked effectively, not an easy task in a large organisation*).

Do be aware that the existence of this sort of an agreement won't necessarily protect your organisation should one of your employees fail to comply with it; however, if the agreement is explained to your employees, and if any sanctions attached are also explained, then it will probably strengthen your hand should disciplinary procedures be required, or should leakage of personal data result in a visit from the data protection regulators.

(8) Protecting People

PROTECTING YOUR IDENTITY

It is very easy to leave sufficient information online for people to steal your identity. Typically, for instance, a telephone banking security check will ask for questions such as:

- your age or date of birth;

- your postcode or address;

- your place of birth;

- you mother's maiden name;

- a regular payment you make to your bank.

It can sometimes be easy to find all of these things online.

Birthdays are often very easily found, and indeed advertised, by social media sites encouraging your friends to send you birthday wishes. As birthdays are sometimes required for e-commerce sites as well it makes sense to have a different

'Internet birthday' that you always use (so it is easy to remember).

Displaying your place of birth is often an option in social media sites. If you want to use this option then it is sensible to use a false place of birth or one that is very general such as England or London.

Your postcode and address may well be publicly available via the electoral register although it is possible to elect to keep this private. Similarly going 'ex-directory' on the telephone may offer some protection to people who still have landlines. It may also be available via the Companies House website if you are a director of your own company. You can make it harder for people to find this by not using your home address as the registered company address (instead you may be able to use your accountant's address).

Your mother's maiden name will be hard to protect if you, or a relative, are a keen user of genealogy sites. If that is the case then you might want to register a different 'mother's maiden name' with banking and other privacy sensitive services that are likely to use this information. Of course you will have to remember this so this does take some effort. (But keeping yourself safe and private online does unfortunately take some effort.)

You might think that 'a regular payment' would be hard for anyone to find online. But this will depend on your habits. For instance if you regularly attend a particular gym and post pictures about this on social media people may guess that you have a subscription to that gym. The same could be true of a church you attend. And of course many people make regular payments (council tax) to their local council which will be fairly easy to uncover. There is probably not much you can do about this, which is why protecting as much other information as possible is very necessary.

PHISHING

Phishing is a scam that uses email (and sometimes SMS and other types of online communication such as social media) to fool people into visiting a fraudulent website or parting with personal information such as passwords and login details. It is a growing problem.

A few years ago phishing emails were relatively easy to spot, often being filled with spelling mistakes and grammatical errors. These emails were sent out to thousands of people, on the basis that at least some people would be fooled. They often referred to a commercial service (such as a bank) that at least a proportion of the recipients would use. Now, though, phishing scams are getting more professional and often target people in a particular company with credible emails that appear to come from a colleague ('spear-phishing') or prominent individuals (such as company CEOs) where it is easy to gather personal information in order to construct a credible scam.

Your organisation may well use a cyber security service that will block out most phishing emails. However, it is possible some will still get through. As that is the case it is worth being vigilant. Here are some guidelines that will help you and your colleagues avoid being phished:

- Never respond to emails that request personal financial information or corporate login details. Be very wary of any email that asks for your password or account information and check that it really comes from the person who claims to have sent it (talk to them, don't just reply to the email!) and that they are authorised to ask for this information.

- Be very wary of emails from banks and other commercial organisations that provide links to 'account maintenance' pages. Banks and e-commerce companies do not usually send such emails. As a rule it is sensible not to click on any links in emails unless you are absolutely sure who they are from (and that can only ever be when someone has told you they have sent you an email). Instead go to the site by typing the URL of the company into your browser and looking for the relevant page (ideally don't cut and paste the URL as it may be subtly different from the one you expect for instance 'L1oyds.com' rather than Lloyds.com').

- Look for signs that an email is 'phishy'. Heading may include substitute characters (e.g. '1nf0rmation') in an attempt to bypass anti-spam software. Alarming claims such as 'Your account numbers have been stolen' may be made. Sometimes (less common these days) there may be spelling mistakes or grammatical errors.

- If you think an email is phishy avoid opening it as this will tell the scammer your email address is valid and you will get more scam emails.

- Keep your browser up to date with the latest security patches as these may help identify and screen out the most common phishing scams.

You should also encourage people to report suspicious activity. If people receive an email they suspect isn't genuine, they should forward it to the spoofed organisation. Many companies have a dedicated email address for reporting such abuse. In addition they should tell your IT department who should in turn forward this information on to their cyber security provider.

Case Study: Phishing Causes a Massive Stock Market Fall

In early 2013 the US stock market suddenly plunged, erasing $140 billion of value from the S&P 500 Index. This wasn't a random blip. The markets were responding to a frightening tweet from Associated Press (AP), a respected news agency, that the White House had been bombed and the president of the USA had been injured. America was under attack.

Except that it wasn't. An organisation called the Syrian Electronic Army had sent the tweet out, having gained control of the Twitter account of a journalist working for AP via a phishing scam. (Grabbing control of someone's Twitter account is, somewhat tiresomely, known as tweet-jacking.) The scam was delivered via a credible email that seemed to be from another AP staffer. This type of highly targeted phishing scam is known as 'spear-phishing'.

To their credit AP had picked up on the scam and had circulated staff about it earlier. But, as terrorists say, you only need to be lucky once.

The incident prompted Twitter to expedite the development of two-factor authentication. Any organisation with a Twitter account should take advantage of this to protect themselves against tweet-jacking. It is, however, harder to defend against phishing.

As phishing is getting more and more of a threat one thing that can be useful to do is run a simulation in order to give people a taste of spear-phishing. You could send your colleagues a targeted spear-phishing email using an outside email address. Ideally dig up some information on their social media sites (Facebook, Twitter, LinkedIn, etc.) and use this to make the email seem credible.

If this is impractical, for instance if you work for a large company, one thing you might do is find out which bank people's pay is sent to. Send them a fake phishing message seemingly from that bank. When they click on the link tell them that they have been phished and give them some tips about avoiding this in future.

Several security consultancies will run phishing simulations for a fee if you want to be sure that the simulation is realistic and ethically conducted.

USING PUBLIC COMPUTERS

Never access a password-protected account (especially your bank or your employer's network) via public computers (e.g. computers in libraries, hotel business centres and Internet cafes) as keylogging software (software that takes a record of all your keystrokes) may be installed.

Alternatively you may simply be at risk from someone 'shoulder surfing' i.e. observing the user names and passwords you type in.

In an emergency, if you need to use a public computer to access a file on a work network (perhaps you have lost your phone and laptop) it will be more sensible to email a colleague and ask them to send it to you, rather than accessing the work network from the public computer.

Of course in theory this puts your email account at risk so you might want to use an unimportant personal email address, or set up a temporary email address (ideally you would do this before leaving the office and tell a colleague about it).

If you do use an important email address, remember to change the password as soon as you can get access to a secure computer.

Case Study: DarkHotel and Travelling Executives

Cyber criminals have been targeting travelling executives to steal sensitive data for 4 years, according to a security firm Kaspersky Lab report in late 2014. The 'DarkHotel' campaign has infected hotel networks with spying software that then infect the computers of hotel guests when they connect to the hotel wi-fi network.

The scam works by tricking the visitors into installing malware by disguising it as updates for common software such as Adobe Flash. The malware then searches for passwords and login credentials as well as sensitive corporate data.

The cyber criminals target precisely, attacking specific executives. They do not go after the same target twice. Their tools are only uploaded to hotel networks at the time of an attack and then deleted, making discovery more difficult.

Defence comprises using a VPN to connect, as well as avoidance of implementing software updates via hotel wi-fi networks.

PUBLIC WI-FI

There are considerable risks to connecting your laptop, tablet or mobile phone to the Internet via public wi-fi. These include connecting to malicious wi-fi services that are masquerading as official wi-fi. The operators of malicious wi-fi services may skim off details such as your account logins or bank details.

See the next chapter (section on using public wi-fi) for details of this.

KEEPING YOUR LOCATION PRIVATE

Your location can be sensitive. You may not want a competitor to know you are visiting a particular supplier or perhaps the target of an acquisition bid. On a personal level it is unwise to tell burglars that you are away from home. And you may not want your children to advertise their location in a local park. However, using a mobile device can mean information about location leaks out.

There are some precautions you can take to prevent this from happening:

- Advise people not to geotag photographs they upload. Most smartphones will tag any photograph that is taken with its location unless you switch this feature off. This means that if the photograph is uploaded to the Internet (to an Instagram page, for instance) someone viewing it may be able to see where it was taken. Learn from Tyrell Jones of Minneapolis who is reported to have posted a photograph of a warehouse where he stored his drugs.

Unfortunately for Jones, he geotagged the location of the photo, leading police directly to him.

- Take care when and how you tweet for your company. If you have been sent somewhere, say an overseas conference, and you tweet about it from your personal account, you are telling people where you are. Rather than do this, tweet from a corporate account.

- Don't advertise your location to other people on social media applications such as TripIt and Foursquare.

- Don't post reviews of overseas hotels on Tripadvisor while you are still there and don't post pictures of your trip on Facebook until you get home.

- Make sure you choose appropriate privacy options in your social media accounts. You probably don't want everybody in the world knowing your business, and making deductions about what you may be doing. But you may also not want all your so-called friends on social media knowing this. (On average people have around 300 Facebook friends but only around 30 true friends. That means they are telling 270 people who are not really their friends what they are doing unless they have edited their privacy settings appropriately).

- Many phone apps and websites such as Google will use your location to 'provide you with better services' (which generally means targeting advertising at you). Switch this option off. Keeping it on means that it can be possible for people to work out where you are likely to be at a particular time from your regular patterns of travel.

(9) Keeping Data Secure outside the Office

KEEPING MOBILE PHONES SAFE

PHYSICAL SECURITY

It sounds obvious but the first place to start is to keep mobile devices physically secure. A mobile phone can be worth well over £100 to a thief. So think of your mobile phone as money and take basic care of it. Don't leave your phone on display on cafe tables where people pass by. And avoid using it in the street for finding directions, unless it is kept close to your body: always be aware of the people around you when using a mobile device.

SECURING DATA ON MOBILE PHONES

If your mobile device is stolen you should be confident that the information on it is secure. It is a good idea to *assume that it will be stolen* and take precautions accordingly. This can involve the following ideas: which ones you choose to follow will depend on your appetite for risk.

Use anti-virus and firewall software for mobile devices and keep it up to date.

Most mobile phones have two levels of protection: device encryption and a lock screen. Use both of these protections: the intention is not to make the phone unbreakable but simply to make it hard to break and give you time, once you have discovered its loss (which is likely to be quickly as most people keep their mobile phone on them all the time) to call your telco and stop the phone from being used.

Use a strong lock screen code such as a password; it is probably best to avoid using a finger swipe pattern such as an 'X' as people can sometimes detect these through grease patterns on the screen. Instead use a pin of at least eight non-obvious numbers (i.e. not 111111 or 12345678) or better still an eight-character password containing letters and numbers. Do remember that you will need to use the password quite frequently so you will need to balance security with convenience.

Ensure the device as a whole is encrypted so that people cannot get access to it if it is stolen. You should switch off the device completely if it is not being used for a time while travelling (if the device hasn't been switched off when it is stolen then people may just need to break through the lock screen).

Ideally, never store critically important information, such as lists of customer details, on a mobile phone or other mobile device.

Ensure any critically important or confidential information that is stored on a mobile phone is well encrypted with a strong password. Be aware of the practical implications of encrypting data on mobile phones. Some encrypted files may be impossible to open on some devices using certain apps. For instance on my Android phone, encrypted Microsoft Word files cannot be opened using the QuickOffice app that allows me to edit them; they can be opened using the Polaris Viewer app – and that doesn't allow me to edit them. If that's a problem – and if you don't want to risk the data leaking – you may have to accept that saving the file to a phone may not be the best solution: you may need a laptop instead.

Avoid automated data backup on mobile phones; ensure this option is unselected in the devices settings.

Make sure your device doesn't store passwords to your accounts so that a thief doesn't need a password to log in. Make sure you actively log out of all your accounts when you finish using them

For sites that offer it, like Twitter and Facebook, employ two-factor authentication to increase security; this means that to log in, as well as your username and password you will also need a code that the platform sends you typically via SMS to your mobile phone. (You can switch this off for 'safe' devices such as your home and office computer.)

Disable wi-fi and Bluetooth when they are not in use on your phone. These can be ways in to your phone. And take care with public wi-fi: ideally you should avoid it but if you need to then only use encrypted wi-fi that needs an access code (see the section on public wi-fi below).

Be circumspect about what you look at using your mobile devices as it may well not be as well protected as your corporate IT network. For instance avoid accessing websites via QR codes (2-dimensional bar codes) – they may be fraudulent and you can't read their address before you go there. Avoid downloading apps from risky places such as little-known websites (even if they are cool): stick to standard stores like Google Play and Apple iTunes where there is a greater degree of protection.

You may also choose to use a phone tracking app on your mobile devices: you might even be able to get it back if you are lucky. Don't rely on them, though, as they can be circumvented relatively easily.

Case Study: The Smartphone Honey Trap

Security software firm Symantec ran an interesting study on how likely it would be that corporate data stored on a 'lost' smartphone would be accessed. Fifty specially formatted smartphones were deliberately lost across North America in places like restaurants, stations and shopping malls. As finders picked up each device and attempted to access apps and data on them, details of those events were centrally logged.

Unsurprisingly perhaps, the researchers found that:

- 96 per cent of lost smartphones were accessed by the finders of the devices.

- 89 per cent of devices were accessed for personal-related apps and information.

- 83 per cent of devices were accessed for corporate-related apps and information.

- 70 per cent of devices were accessed for both business and personal-related apps and information.

Slightly more encouragingly 50 per cent of smartphone finders contacted the owner and provided contact.

WHAT TO DO IF YOUR PHONE IS LOST OR STOLEN

If you do manage to lose your phone then you will need to get in touch with your telecoms provider who should be able to inactivate the SIM or even the phone to stop illegal voice and data calls being made. Again it sounds obvious but you should do this as soon as possible: huge bills can be (and are) racked up by people who fail to tell their telecoms provider about lost mobile phones. In October 2014 a teacher who failed to tell Vodafone for 4 days about a phone lost in Spain was presented with a £15,000 bill.

Keep a note of the phone's IMEI number. Get this by dialling *#06# on your phone. It will help your telecoms provider to immobilise your phone should it be stolen.

In addition to telling your telecoms provider, you should also tell your IT manager as he or she may be able to detect and prevent unauthorised incursions into the corporate IT system via the lost device.

And finally, do remember that your passwords may have been compromised, especially if you allow automatic access to things like email and Twitter. Even if the thieves can't see the password, if they are logged into your account they can change it, locking you out of your accounts. So it is a good idea to change any passwords you feel may be at risk as soon as possible.

REMOTE LOCKING AND DATA WIPING

It is a sensible idea to insist that BYOD device owners install an app that will delete the data if the incorrect password is input too many times. Require the use of a strong password to secure personal devices that have access to corporate data. Instruct BYOD owners to install an app that will lock the device if the incorrect password is input too many times or if it is inactive for a time.

If sensitive documents, such as work emails, are stored on a mobile phone then it is also sensible to consider installing some form of data wiping application. These work in two ways: either by wiping data if an incorrect password is input too many times, or by allowing the owner to go online to a website where the instruction to wipe the data can be given. Consider making this obligatory for people who access and store work information on their mobile phone. This can often be achieved on a phone-by-phone basis, depending on the manufacturer. Or you can use mobile device management software that will allow remote wiping and locking of personal devices from a central control point.

USING THE INTERNET

Don't assume that using the Internet on a mobile device is as safe as it is when you are using a laptop. Take basic precautions about what you access.

Make sure your mobile device has adequate and up-to-date security protection (a firewall and virus checker) from a reputable company; this should be an obligation for anyone using a mobile device for work purposes.

If you are going to use public wi-fi for shopping (and it isn't really advisable to do this) then make sure that any site you use has 'https' (not 'http') at the start of the address. This means it is more likely to be a secure and encrypted site.

If your mobile phone browser warns you that a site has an untrusted security certificate then don't connect to it.

Take care when clicking on adverts or text links; depending on the device you are using it may be impossible to see where the link is leading to; given the rise in malvertising (advertising that leads to malicious sites or downloads malicious code if you click on it), and the fact that many mobile devices are less well protected from malvertising than laptops and desktop computers, you may be putting yourself at extra risk.

USING PUBLIC WI-FI

Even if you take care to hold on to your mobile devices, the information on them will be at risk whenever you are outside your home or the office. One way you can put it at risk by using public wi-fi services to connect to the Internet. It is true that these risks can be hard to manage, but they are impossible if you are unaware of them.

Take care when using public wi-fi (e.g. in coffee shops, hotels and at conferences) and don't assume it is secure: there may be a hacker at the next desk to you (a 'man in the middle') who is happily siphoning off all your data. Here are some tips for keeping safe:

- Never use public wi-fi for sensitive tasks like banking or accessing your corporate network.

- Turn off wi-fi on your mobile device when not using it: if you don't, your phone may connect automatically to a wi-fi service exposing you to risk.

- Sign up for a reputable VPN service: this will act as a barrier between you and the public wi-fi, adding a layer of extra security. Asking people to remember to turn wi-fi off all the time they are out of the office or home environment may not work as they are likely to forget and a VPN service will provide some protection when they do forget.

- If you are planning to use public wi-fi, check out the name first. Your mobile device will be able to show you a list of wi-fi hot spots available: you need to select a hot spot you can trust. Increasingly, criminals are setting up their own wi-fi services that mimic public wi-fi by using credible names or words like 'Free wi-fi'.These are sometimes called 'evil twins'. If you are in a venue of some sort, a cafe, shop or conference, the official wi-fi will have a name: if you don't know what it is, ask. And if you are using public wi-fi such as BT's wi-fi service make sure you know exactly how it should appear on your mobile: according to BT's website (at the time of writing) you should see 'BT wi-fi', 'BT Openzone' or 'BT FON' so if you see something like 'Free BT wi-fi' you should avoid it.

- Instead of public wi-fi, use your mobile telco's 3G or 4G data connection. Or simply wait until you get in range of a wi-fi service you trust (your home or office network).

Case Study: Ethical Hackers and the Evil Twin

Do you use public wi-fi to connect your mobile device to the Internet? If you do you may well be putting yourself at risk. This isn't a theoretical threat.

In 2013 ethical ('white hat') hackers employed by Trend Micro set up a fake wi-fi service in a park in central London using a smartphone. It was set up so that all data heading to and from the wi-fi hotspot passed through their laptop first.

They had no trouble getting 'customers'. That wasn't the surprise. What was surprising was the data that they could capture. For instance user names and passwords were easily available, and even bank details where people accessed major e-commerce sites.

Several apps that allowed the team to grab usernames, passwords and contact lists of smartphone owners who connected to their hotspot were freely available on the Google Play Store.

SENSIBLE HOUSEKEEPING

There are some other things you should consider to keep information safe on mobile devices.

Require separate access credentials for personal devices and work-based desktop computers. Limit the access that personal devices can have to those parts of the network their owners need to do their jobs when working remotely.

Instruct device owners that if personal devices that are used for work purposes break or become obsolete they need to be returned to IT department for data cleaning before being repaired or disposed of. This should be written into your BYOD User Agreement (see Chapter 7).

Make sure you back up any data that you have created on the mobile device (such as photographs or other documents): you don't want them lost along with your device.

PROTECTING MOBILE DATA STORAGE

As well as their mobile phones, laptops and tablets, people who are working outside their normal office may have portable data stores such as CDs and USB sticks. These also need to be protected. There is less you can do (and less you need to do as these devices have much less functionality than a mobile phone) but you do need to ensure that any sensitive data on them is encrypted appropriately.

Case Study: Manchester Police and the Lost USB Sticks

In 2012 Manchester Police were fined £150,000 by the Information Commissioner's Office (ICO) for losing personal data. The action was taken as a result of the theft from an officer's home of a memory stick containing sensitive personal data. The data included details of more than a thousand people with links to serious crime investigations. The device had no password protection.

Lax security was endemic at the time. The ICO found that officers across the force regularly used unencrypted memory sticks. It appeared that data was regularly copied from police computers in order to access it away from the office.

Assistant Chief Constable Lynne Potts said: 'This was very much an isolated incident.' However, despite a similar security breach in September 2010, the Manchester Police had failed to implement restrictions on downloading information and had failed to train staff sufficiently in data protection and safe data storage and transport.

Portable storage devices can be very useful, however, as they can be used to keep sensitive data separate from laptops or phones. A small USB stick or a small CD will be unobtrusive and of little value and therefore unlikely to catch a thief's attention.

⑩ Social Media Risk

Social media is not yet generally recognised as a major issue for cyber security. Many people think 'Social media: that's for the PR department to manage, isn't it?' In fact the dangers from social media can be found in every part of your organisation, from the board to the HR department.

And there is one vital thing to realise. Social media possesses these risks to your organisation *whether or not your organisation uses social media.* Even if you don't have a corporate Twitter account and a Facebook page your organisation can be at risk: because even if you don't use it, you can be sure that your employees and your customers do use it.

Handled badly, social media can cause enormous damage to organisations. And that's why understanding social media risk is a very important part of cyber security.

WHAT IS SOCIAL MEDIA RISK

Social media risk is the risk of people causing damage to your organisation on social media platforms such as Facebook and

Twitter. There are risks from consumers who say unpleasant things about your organisation, brands, products or employees. There are also risks that employees, who can be identified as employees, say things on social media that reflect badly on your organisation. And there are risks that hackers use social media as a way of penetrating your information networks.

Case Study: Centcom Social Media Hack

January 2015 saw a very embarrassing hack: the US Defence Central Command (Centcom) Twitter and YouTube accounts were hacked. The hackers posted messages and images that supported Islamic State.

The hacks were downplayed as 'cyber vandalism' by the US government who stated that there was no security risk and no classified information had been posted.

Of course the computers that host Twitter and YouTube don't have any connection to the US Central Command computers so a security leak via Twitter couldn't have happened.

But the incident is nonetheless concerning. Apart from the fact that it was a massive propaganda coup for Islamic State supporters, many people who don't understand the relationship between Twitter accounts and Centcom's systems may well have been very concerned, undermining trust in the agency. More importantly, the incident shows that cyber security is not being taken as seriously as it might by US government agencies.

Most concerning of all though is the fact that if hackers managed to guess the passwords of Centcom social media accounts they may be able to guess the passwords of more sensitive Centcom accounts. Over half of all Internet users confess to using the same password across multiple accounts. We have to hope that's not a security risk for the US government.

REPUTATIONAL DAMAGE

Reputational damage from social media can happen in several ways.

REPUTATIONAL DAMAGE BY HACKERS

It can happen when weak passwords result in corporate social media accounts being hijacked. For instance Burger King's Twitter account was hijacked by people who posted that 'Burger King just got sold to McDonalds'.

Case Study: Burger King and Reputational Risk

The most common Twitter password in 2012 was '111111'. Not so difficult to hack. Whether or not this was Burger King's Twitter password in early 2013, their account was hacked by mischief makers. The usual messages about new restaurants and special offers were replaced by a series of strange tweets and the profile photo was replaced by a background of Fish McBites and the Golden Arches logo with a profile description that read in part 'Burger King USA official Twitter account. Just got sold to McDonalds because the whopper flopped'. It wasn't all bad news for Burger King, though. Following this attack, and the social media attention it generated, Burger King added an extra 30,000 followers.

REPUTATIONAL DAMAGE BY MARKETERS

Social media marketing is a new discipline. And not everyone gets it right all the time. There have been many instances of enthusiastic marketers and PR people using social media to enhance the reputations of their organisations and having the opposite effect.

Search for "social media fails" online and you will get a number of stories, many amusing. Sometimes it is obvious why things went wrong. For instance when in April 2014 the New York Police Department posted a picture of a happy New Yorker flanked by a couple of burly cops and encouraged Twitter users to send in their pictures of experiences with the NYPD, not all the pictures posted were complimentary!

Perhaps they should have seen that coming. The sensitive antennae of social media users can be ruffled all too easily. For example in May 2015 Spotify was accused of sexism and ageism when it tweeted the question 'How would you explain Spotify to your mom?' as part of a Mothers' Day promotion.

REPUTATIONAL DAMAGE BY EMPLOYEES

Reputational damage can also happen when weak control of access to corporate social media accounts means that malicious or mischievous employees can post inappropriate content without fear of discovery. This is a substantial risk. When many employees have access to the corporate social media accounts, there is often no way to know who has posted what. This may well have been what happened when the British Labour Party inexplicably posted a policy initiative that promised everyone a 'free owl'. Strict access controls or a single sign-on system help to control this risk.

Case Study: Labour Promises Free Owls for All

In the summer of 2014 the UK's Labour Party tweeted (hooted?) the promise of free owls for all with a post on Twitter that read 'Everyone should have his own owl'. The tweet was quickly deleted and luckily the odd promise didn't ruffle too many feathers. Nonetheless it did demonstrate a failure to control the content on their social media accounts.

The incident was blamed on a 'bot' (a software package that performs automated tasks on the Internet). But it could well have happened because an inappropriate (or possibly badly trained) person within the PR team had anonymous access to the Twitter account.

If the author was a hacker then a stronger password protocol would have prevented the problem; if a mischievous member of the PR team then education combined with a single sign-on protocol that would allow the author to be tracked might have worked.

The gaffe would have been very hard to prevent using automatic moderation (moderation in this case means the editing and if necessary deleting of posts that contain inappropriate language): the words used are not offensive in any way and don't mention anyone by name. (Human moderation might not be appropriate for a political party wanting to be able to respond very rapidly to events as they unroll.)

Reputational damaged is also caused when employees post to the wrong account. There have been a number of cases of employees posting content on their employer's social media accounts when thinking they were posting on their own accounts. This is in fact very easy to do with some social media platforms.

Case Study: Chrysler and New Media Strategies

In March 2014 an employee of marketing agency New Media Strategies posted an expletive-filled tweet 'I find it ironic that Detroit is known as the #motorcity and yet no one here knows how to ... drive'. Unfortunately, rather than posting the tweet on his own Twitter account, he managed to post it by mistake on Chrysler's account. Chrysler promptly sacked New Media Strategies.

Single sign-on systems can help prevent this type of accident. But education (about what is appropriate and what is not) is also important for managing social media risk. Most important though is the development of a social media policy document that spells out acceptable behaviour, identifies unacceptable behaviour, and details sanctions for failure to comply with the policy. This policy document needs to be shared with all employees in such a way that they understand what it means and, importantly, are aware of the sanctions that may apply for non-compliance.

Search 'Social media policy template' for examples of the content of social media policy documents.

REPUTATIONAL DAMAGE BY THIRD PARTIES

Reputational damage can also be caused because inappropriate content that has not been moderated is posted to an organisation's social media accounts. This could be a member of the public using inappropriate language on your corporate Facebook page. Automatic content moderation tools are available that can reduce this risk substantially.

Whatever the nature of posts on corporate social media pages, it is important to respond appropriately to them. A sensible strategy is to employ some form of 'triage': genuine complaints are dealt with rapidly (within 24 hours and ideally within 2 or 3 hours) ideally offline; compliments and constructive comments and suggestions should also be responded to rapidly; the occasional 'troll' (someone out to create unpleasantness for no real reason) should perhaps be ignored; and anything serious such as threat to the safety of customers or company representatives should be dealt with immediately.

Generally the marketing or PR function will be fielding comments from the public. But not all comments from the general public will be relevant to the marketing or PR function. Therefore as well as triaging comments from the public it is important that they are directed to the right people for response. For instance a comment about a potential product improvement should perhaps be directed to a research and development function: where this is done it will be necessary to ensure that the people responsible for replying have some basic understanding of the 'etiquette' of social media as well as a realisation that any response they make will be in the public domain.

DAMAGE TO OPERATIONAL EFFICIENCY

Social media can also cause damage to operational efficiency in several ways.

REDUCED EMPLOYEE PRODUCTIVITY

At its very simplest, the inappropriate use of social media sites can cause a reduction in employee productivity. Some organisations simply ban social media use at work but the reality is that where this happens people will probably access social media via personal devices – or decline to join your organisation.

It may be better to control the inevitable use of social media in other ways. For instance a policy that restricts the use of social media to certain times of day (e.g. lunchtimes) or that allows a limited amount of social media during working hours (say 15 minutes a day maximum) can be supported by a social media usage agreement that informs employees that their use of social media may be monitored in certain circumstances and that they should have no expectation of privacy when using social media at work.

There is probably no need to alter employment contracts to manage the use of social media at work. It is likely that an instruction to avoid using, or limit the use of, social media at work would be regarded as a reasonable management instruction rather than something that needs to be written into an employment contract. Nonetheless it is better to have that sort of instruction in writing, to explain what it means to all employees, and to ensure they are aware of any sanctions (up to dismissal) that may be imposed if the instructions are not complied with.

MALWARE AND DAMAGE TO BUSINESS PROCESSES AND NETWORK SECURITY

Reduced operational efficiency can also be caused by malware (malicious software like viruses) 'caught' via social media. Because many social media sites are riddled with malware, using them can lead to problems such as the infection of computers with viruses that can cause difficulties to business processes through data deletion or slowed computer operations. Malware is commonly present in social media surveys and advertisements which is one reason to restrict the use of social media at work.

The theft of login data by a malicious website masquerading as a genuine one is also a risk. Clicking on an innocuous-looking advert in social media may lead to a site that downloads keylogging software that will compromise network security at a later date.

Another danger from social media is that of 'phishing' where employees are fooled into disclosing important information such as login details by people posing as trusted contacts on social media.

And finally, using social media often involves watching video. On some corporate networks, if too many people are watching video at any one time, computer operations may be significantly slowed, leading to difficulties for other employees.

HR ISSUES

HR processes are surprisingly vulnerable to social media. Companies have been forced to dismiss valued employees who have said inappropriate things on social media. For instance in 2013 PayPal parted company with their Director of Strategy after he was found to have posted some unwise comments about colleagues on Twitter.

In addition companies that read social media profiles of potential recruits have been accused of discrimination. The difficulty here is that social media profiles may highlight things such as race or disability that are not shown on a CV: unsuccessful candidates who have been forced to give access to their social media accounts as part of the recruitment process can accuse the employer of discrimination. To avoid this threat some companies will task an employee with editing a candidate's social media profile so that anything potentially discriminatory (gender, age etc) is deleted; the bowdlerised profile is then handed to the HR department

There are people management issues too. Some organisations may think it appropriate to keep an eye on the social media accounts of their employees. Some managers are persuaded to become 'friends' with juniors on social media. This can lead to all sorts of problems: allegations of privacy infringements as well as discrimination and bullying have all been raised. In my view it is generally best for managers to avoid being 'friends' with juniors on social media.

Perhaps most worrying is the fact that employees sometimes bully other employees online. This behaviour may or may be intended as a joke. But if the victims feel they are being bullied they may well be able to take action against the employer. This is the case whether or not the bullying happens in company time or even on company computers. The principle of vicarious liability may well mean the employers are liable for damages whether or not they have knowingly facilitated the bullying.

LOSS OF ASSETS AND OTHER VALUE

Social media can cause damage to company assets. There is a risk to share price from a badly handled social media incident. As yet this risk remains quite theoretical. One example that people sometimes use is the 'United breaks guitars' story. In this story a musician who felt his guitar had been damaged during a flight wrote a song about the incident and posted it online. The song 'went viral' i.e. it was circulated widely, to millions of people. The airline's share price dropped by around 10 per cent in the days after and some people have linked this to the social media activity.

However, there are other risks to assets that are easier to demonstrate.

Counterfeiting is a real problem on social media where people use their social media accounts to publish unofficial information about a brand in order to sell fake goods.

Strategically valuable information can be accidentally leaked on social media through careless discussions that give away things such as acquisition targets or an intention to purchase a new business system.

Wasted investments can be made when badly thought-out social media campaigns are launched at the expense of more efficient (but less attractive) campaigns in other more traditional channels. As part of this employees who are tasked with building social media assets such as lists of Twitter followers can simply decamp to another employer taking their followers with them if not managed appropriately.

LEGAL PROBLEMS

Perhaps most frightening to many organisations are the legal problems that can be caused through social media. For instance compliance failures can be caused by people failing to apply industry regulation and data protection, advertising and fair trading rules to social media content. This is of particular concern to regulated industries such as financial services and pharmaceuticals who are required to treat (and archive) social media content in the same way that they would other 'conversations' with customers such as email exchanges. But in fact any industry can be caught out by inappropriate marketing activities such as a failure to declare paid endorsements.

Case Study: The NHS and 'Astro Turfing'

The Nottinghamshire Health Care Trust website contains a section devoted to 'reviews' of their service. These are largely positive. Unfortunately for the Trust, in 2013 a BBC investigation uncovered the fact that around 50 per cent of the reviews were submitted from Trust computers, rather than by members of the public. The Trust claimed that the reviews were posted on behalf of patients. Whatever your opinion about the ethics of this, 'astroturfing', the practice of posting reviews about an organisation that you work for or which has paid you to post reviews without declaring your interest, is illegal in a commercial context.

Another problem that social media can exacerbate is the misuse of third-party intellectual property. It may be that an employee shares a copyright photograph or music track via social media. If that employee does so on a social media account that is in some way linked to the employer (for instance if the employee identifies who they work for on their social media profile) then it is possible that the employer would be liable vicariously.

If that sounds unlikely then take the example of Gene Morphis, who was the Finance Director of Fransesca, a clothing company. Using an anonymous Twitter account (in the name of @theoldcfo) he tweeted 'Board meeting. Good numbers=Happy Board.' It was enough to get him fired because he 'improperly communicated company information through social media'. Unfortunately for Mr Morphis, while his Twitter account was anonymous it was linked to sites where he could be identified as Fransesca's CFO including his blog, LinkedIn and Facebook.

It is also possible that losses could be caused when contracts are entered into or varied accidentally on social media. While there don't appear to be any published instances of this happening so far, contracts have certainly been accidentally varied in email exchanges and there is no reason why the same thing shouldn't happen via a social media exchange.

SOCIAL MEDIA RISK FACTORS

It helps to understand why social media is such a risk if you want to manage this risk. It is probably because of a number of factors including:

- Culture: people tend to think of content posted on social media as being in some way unofficial: 'It's only Twitter so why does it matter?'

- Lack of knowledge: People often think that social media content is ephemeral and will disappear quickly. It doesn't: once online content is always online, especially if people share it. RBS banker Rory Cullinan discovered this in March 2015 when he sent Snapchat messages to his daughter about boring board meetings and she reposted them on Instagram, causing him a certain amount of embarrassment.

- Anonymity: 'No one knows you are a dog on the Internet': as it is relatively easy to become anonymous on the Internet, people are often encouraged to be malicious. An example of this was the children's social media site ask.fm which has been accused of causing several suicides as a result on anonymous bullying.

- Speed and reach: the nature of the Internet allows stories to spread rapidly and widely, especially if they are taken up by commercial media sites.

- Private vs professional: People often combine professional social media comments with private social media comments, especially on Twitter; when this happens a malicious private comment made by an employee can reflect badly on the employer.

As with any risk, understanding the motivations behind the people responsible for the risk can help in its management and mitigation.

Case Study: Peter Nunn Finds out that Social Media Matters to the Law

In 2013 a campaign was launched by journalist Caroline Criado-Perez to put the face of Victorian novelist Jane Austen on the £10 note. The campaign was supported by MP Stella Creasy.

Peter Nunn took exception to this campaign and launched a social media 'campaign of hatred' against the two women. It wasn't a big campaign – only six tweets. But the nature of the tweets was highly offensive and threatening. He also retweeted offensive messages.

Mr Nunn was charged under section 127 of the 2003 Communications Act which outlaws messages that are 'grossly offensive or of an indecent, obscene or menacing character'. He claimed that his messages were to exercise his freedom of speech. The judge disagreed and sentenced him to 18 weeks in jail.

DEALING WITH A SOCIAL MEDIA CRISIS

Sometimes bad things that people are saying about your organisation can start to gather momentum. Sometimes the volume of comments can result in the story being taken up by commercial media such as the press and TV. When this happens you are facing a social media crisis that will need careful and prompt management.

Typically the birth of a crisis will be in forums and blogs where posts may only be read by a few people. However, once the issue starts to be discussed on major platforms such as Facebook and Twitter there is a risk that the number of people who hear about the issue will grow. The real danger then is that the issue is amplified and turns into a crisis when commercial online media sites such as AOL or Yahoo! start talking about the issue. If that happens then it is very likely that mainstream offline media – newspapers and TV channels – will broadcast the issue to a very wide audience, and you are then faced with a full blown PR crisis.

If a social media crisis happens you will need to be able to take appropriate action. And to do this, your organisation will need a number of things:

A way of agreeing that a crisis happening or about to happen. Not every unpleasant mention of your brand on social media is a crisis: some simply require a response to the individual who makes the comment and others should be ignored. You might decide to put your crisis plan into action only if mainstream media owners get hold of the story, or if the volume of negative comments about your organisation crosses a certain threshold.

A crisis plan. This will involve agreeing who is responsible for managing the crisis. For instance you may wish to escalate management from the social media team to an appropriately experienced director or to your PR agency. It will also involve identifying likely crisis scenarios up front and developing some pre-prepared holding statements so that you can react immediately.

An experienced crisis team. Managing a social media crisis can be very stressful. Not only can the crisis burst out in various different places (Facebook, Twitter, online communities, blog posts ...) but the nature of comments from the general public can be personally abusive. A team which has experience of a crisis, or which has had the opportunity to practise dealing with a crisis (there are a number of companies who will run a fake social media crisis for your team) will be better able to manage any negative consequences.

(11) Who is Stealing your Organisation's Identity?

There is an expression (taken from a 1993 cartoon in the *New Yorker* magazine): 'On the Internet no one knows you are a dog.' In other words you can pretend to be whoever you want to be and people have no way of knowing whether it is true.

Why is that a problem? Because people can easily pretend that they represent your organisation for their own purposes. And that can result in your organisation or its brands being damaged in a number of ways, including reputational damage and reduced sales.

MONITORING IDENTITY

How can people hijack your identity? In a number of ways. Let's consider that well-known industrial conglomerate, the Trumpton Widget Manufacturing Company (corporate motto 'Widgets when and where you need them'). Their website is www.trumptonwidgets.com. They don't have a blog or any social media accounts.

Unfortunately a disaffected employee wants to damage the company and has set up a website www.trumpton-widgets. com (with a hyphen) where he posts damaging information about the company. He also has a blog using the popular blogging platform blogsRus, with the URL trumpton-widgets-suck.blogsrus.com. And he has a Twitter account designed to do the same thing with the Twitter handle @trumptonwidgets.

Trumpton Widgets have missed a trick in failing to register the hyphenated URL and the Twitter account (and no doubt several other social media accounts). This would have helped them defend their name. They may be able to ask Twitter to stop the employee using the @trumptonwidgets name. But there isn't much they can do about the trumpton-widgets-suck blog, although being aware of it, and monitoring it for lies and libels, would be sensible.

In fact people can use many things to hijack your identity in the form of your organisational or brand names, your logos, and your straplines, including:

• website URLs;

• social media accounts;

• search-engine advertisements;

• listings in online directories;

• email addresses.

How do you guard against this? Well, the first thing to do is to monitor the Internet. It isn't always sufficient to monitor just for your organisation's name, though. Depending on your appetite for risk, you may also want to monitor for mentions of:

- your brand names;

- the names of the CEO and other senior executives;

- the use of your strapline;

- the use of your logo.

You can set up monitoring in a number of ways. The simplest is to set up search-engine alerts (such as Google Alerts) to tell you when particular words or combinations of words are used online. However, while this is useful, you won't necessarily be notified of all new instances and, in particular, any existing instances of the words being used won't be shown to you.

In order to show existing usages, then run some simple search-engine searches. There are particular types of search you can run, for instance looking for phrases such as your straplines or instances of a word appearing within a URL.

If you are particularly concerned about people using your name in social media (and perhaps you should be) then you might want to subscribe to a 'buzz monitoring' service that looks out for mentions of a particular word or phrase when used on social media sites like Twitter and Facebook, in blogs and in community discussion forums. These tools range from free to several hundred thousand pounds a year. As with most things, you get what you pay for.

An alternative is to subscribe to a 'Point of Presence' monitoring service that will trawl the Internet for the words and phrases you are looking for. The benefit of these services is that they will sometimes go 'deeper' than standard search engines and buzz monitoring tools, pulling out results from social media accounts as well the wider Internet. This can be particularly helpful if you are trying to manage what independent salespeople are saying (and promising) about your products on social media as some of these tools can confirm whether a mention of your brand is combined with required wording such as 'investments can go down as well as up'.

PREVENTING A HIJACK

As well as monitoring who is saying what about your brands, it is also helpful to prevent people using your brand names wherever possible. Of course you may have access to legal remedies if someone 'passes off' a website as belonging to you. However, stopping it happening in the first place is a lot easier. In order to do this, identify potential URLs that hijackers than can use and register them if possible. The more at risk you are, the more you will want do this. For instance a bank, potentially a target for scammers, may want to register more alternative URLs than a small shop. URLs to consider registering include:

- non-standard URL suffixes (known as TLDs or Top Level Domains) such as .biz, .net, .org, .eu (there are now many new URL suffixes available);

- common misspellings such as TrumtonWidgets (without the p);

- hyphens and other additions such as Trumpton-Widgets, TrumptonWidgets1 and TrumptonWidgetsLtd;

- obviously fraudulent versions of your URL such as TrumptonW1dgets;

- 'Anti' URLs such as TrumptonWidgetsSucks and IHateTrumptonWidgets.

In addition register appropriate social media accounts in your brands' names in particular for Facebook, YouTube, Twitter, LinkedIn, Instagram, Google+ and Pinterest. This will prevent other people from using the most obvious social media account names.

Do remember that it will be impossible to prevent every single abusive use of your organisation's and brands' names in URLs and social media accounts so monitoring, and taking appropriate action when you find something, is essential.

DEALING WITH FAKE SITES AND HATE SITES

If someone does set up fake sites with the intention of damaging your reputation, then you have two strategies to consider.

GENERATING VISIBILITY

First try to make the fake sites as unobtrusive as possible on search engines, so that people don't see them.

This means making your websites appear as high up search-engine results as possible. Ideally you want your website to appear on the first page of results and the rival's website to appear on the second page (or lower). Alternatively you just want your website to appear above the rival website.

You can try to do this by employing two tactics. First make sure that you have the relevant websites and social media accounts set up. Websites like LinkedIn and YouTube get huge amounts of traffic so your accounts on these sites (e.g. www.linkedin.com/company/trumptonwidgets) are likely to appear above hate sites like trumptonwidgetsucks and fake sites with little traffic such as Trumpton-widgets.com. If you have several of these sites (i.e. for all the major social media sites), plus a blog, a Wikipedia page and perhaps entries on relevant industry directories, and if your own sites rank well, you will have a good chance of pushing the hate sites and fake sites off the first page of results.

In order to maintain the search-engine ranking of these defensive sites you will have to treat them seriously by ensuring they have some content and that their content is renewed every so often. So for instance, your YouTube account should have a new video added to it every month or so. This might sound like a nuisance but it is a sensible thing to be doing for marketing purposes as well as in order to defend against hate sites and fake sites.

Some people advocate using 'negative SEO' tactics to damage these rival websites and push them further down search-engine listings. Negative SEO tactics involve doing things that Google 'disapproves' of and is likely to penalise a website for. This can include buying lots of low-quality links to a website from 'link farms' and creating lots of new websites that duplicate the content of the website you are trying to damage. This tactic is generally considered unwise: as well as being unethical it can backfire and result in damage to your own website.

TAKING LEGAL ACTION

The other option that is open to you is to take legal action. While this is probably going to be necessary if you discover someone who has set up a website to sell counterfeit versions of your goods, you might want to think twice about taking legal action against a disaffected employee or an unhappy customer.

Apart from being expensive, this can make your company look like an uncaring bully. In many cases the better approach is to negotiate with the offending persons, pointing out perhaps that they are offending against copyright rules (if they are) and, especially if they are unhappy customers, offering reparations.

DEALING WITH FAN SITES

If people like your products they may well set up sites that praise them. In doing so they may well use copyright material such as logos and other IP.

The default response of many lawyers in these cases is to issue some sort of 'cease and desist' letter, threatening the fans with legal action if they don't stop abusing your copyright material.

While it is important to defend your copyright material, there are more constructive ways of going about this that threatening to sue your fans. In perhaps the most famous example of a company being constructive about fan sites, the

Coca Cola Company engaged with two of their fans who had set up a Facebook page about Coca Cola. Rather than insisting on deleting or taking over the page themselves, they worked with the fans to provide them with extra information and to support their fan page. The result was, and still is, a very successful Facebook page that benefits Coca Cola hugely.

⑫ Disposing of Data Safely

How many new computers, laptops and smartphones have you had over the last few years?

Moore's Law dictates that computer technology doubles in power (or halves in price) every 18 months. That means that computing equipment becomes obsolete fairly rapidly. Older equipment may be recycled to a more junior colleague or a colleague with simpler requirements. Or it may be dispensed with totally, perhaps being sold outside the company or simply thrown away.

If a computer is being taken outside the organisation, or used by a colleague with fewer information access privileges, it is important to ensure that all the data on it is erased.

The trouble is, erasing data isn't as easy as it might first appear. For instance simply 'deleting' files on a computer's hard disk doesn't necessarily delete them. They may still be available somewhere on the hard disk and even if they are not available as coherent files, parts of them may still be available and capable of being reconstructed.

HOW TO DISPOSE OF DATA

DESTROYING DISKS

The simplest and most certain way to make sure no one can access data on an unwanted computer is to destroy the hard disks. Many companies offer hard-disk shredding services – or you could just take a hammer to it. Of course this makes the computer unusable and for many people this will be unacceptable, given that older computers are still going to be useful to many people who perhaps just want simple word-processing software and Internet access.

However, for computers that once contained sensitive personal or commercial data destroying the disks may be the best route. An alternative is to 'degauss' the disk which involves removing the magnetic charge which holds the data. This also renders the disk, and thus the computer, unusable, although of course there are likely to be parts that can be recycled.

DELETING DATA

Alternatively you may decide to wipe all the data from the hard disk. As mentioned above 'deleting' files (even if your 'bin' file is subsequently also cleared) won't necessarily mean the data is cleared from the disk.

Similarly don't think that 'reformatting' the disk will work. This merely clears all the location data from the disk meaning that the computer operating system can't find it. But the data is still there and a clever programmer will be able to locate it.

Instead you need to use data destruction software. This is a program that is designed to overwrite the data on the disk several times with 0s and 1s, making it almost (note the 'almost') impossible to read. Different programs will overwrite the data a different number of times – the more often the data is overwritten the harder it will be to decipher.

Data destruction programs are available free and overwriting the data in this way is fine for most purposes, although perhaps not if you are a national government with particularly sensitive secrets. Before you do this, remember to save any files that you want to keep.

If you are recycling the computer internally you may instead want simply to delete certain files. Again, remember that deleting them won't delete them totally. Even if you drop them in your computer's trash bin and then empty the trash bin, the files will still be hanging around somewhere. Again you need special software, this time software that lets you select individual files and over write them. Once you have done that you can prepare the computer for its next owner.

If files need to be destroyed for reasons of regulatory compliance then it will be sensible to use a commercial (paid for) product that guarantees data destruction: the free programs, although fine for most purposes, will not guarantee you anything and may fail to delete certain types of file.

Case Study: The NHS and a Failure to Protect Personal Data

In 2012 the Brighton and Sussex University Hospitals NHS Trust was fined £325,000 by the Information Commissioner's Office (ICO) following a serious breach of the Data Protection Act (DPA).

The fine followed the discovery of highly sensitive personal data on hard drives sold on eBay in October and November 2010. The data included details of medical conditions, disability living allowance forms and children's reports refering to tens of thousands of patients and staff.

The breach occurred when the Trust's IT service provider was asked to destroy 1,000 hard drives. The drives were kept in a locked room and a contractor was given supervised access to the room to destroy the drives. However, despite the supervision, a large number of hard drives destined for destruction were removed from the hospital rather than being destroyed.

It is believed that the contractor could not gain access to the room unsupervised. However, it is also acknowledged that the contractor would have left the building for breaks and that the hospital is publicly accessible. Was the room left open while the contractor was out allowing unauthorised people to enter? No one knows but what is clear is that the security processes that were put in place were either inadequate or were not followed.

IT waste disposal is a complex issue: it is not remotely sufficient to delete files or even reformat disks. The lesson here is that employing an IT waste disposal company that is accredited with ISO 27001 is an important step. Although of course, if doors to unoccupied rooms are left open, then things are likely to 'walk'!

CLEANING PORTABLE DEVICES

You may also need to clean portable drives like USBs. Again you could just use a hammer but if you want to use them again then you may prefer to wipe the files. Use file destruction software, making sure that the disks you select for destruction are on the portable disk and not on your computer. Note that this process can take quite a while.

If you have some CDs or DVDs with data you want to erase, the chances are you won't be able to use file destruction software unless they are rewritable disks. If they are not, you will have to destroy them. Wear safety glasses and simply snip them into pieces with a pair of scissors or if you are particularly risk-averse use a commercially available disk shredding device (like a paper shredder but more powerful).

CLEANING SMARTPHONES

Disposing of smartphones safely is also important, especially if they are being sold or recycled, but even if they are being passed on to a family member.

This is a particular security issue as these devices may have been used to access corporate information (e.g. lists of email contacts) or a corporate social media account, but if they are personally owned devices they may have been less subject to your information security processes.

Again, it is not sufficient to delete the files and even resetting the phone back to factory settings won't delete the data. You will need to identify appropriate data destruction software. For instance, for Android devices there are a number of free utilities available from the Google Play Store.

In the case of BYOD security (where the smartphone is owned and managed by an individual employee rather than your organisation) you will need to educate the device owners about the need to delete the data properly when are given access to corporate data in the first place. If they have ever bought anything on the phone or used it for banking then they will probably be grateful for the information. And if you are really worried about information leakage, offer to wipe their phones for free before they dispose of them, or make this a condition of accessing corporate data on the device.

⑬ The Internet of Things

The Internet of Things (as opposed to the original Internet, sometimes called the Internet of People) refers to the way that devices such as factory machines, security cameras, heating and lighting systems, lifts, and even cars are connected to other devices or computers via the Internet.

Devices that connect to the Internet are often called 'smart devices' and they are here to stay. But as more and more devices are connected to the Internet (it is already billions) what are the issues for security?

At first sight, it doesn't seem likely that increasing security, for instance putting a smart security camera over the front entrance to your office, is adding to risk rather than reducing it. But it may be. For instance when the US government first started to use RFID (Radio Frequency Identification) tags to increase security in passports is was discovered that the data could be read from 10 metres away with equipment available on eBay for a few hundred dollars.

NETWORK SECURITY

The most obvious risk from devices that are connected to the Internet is one of network security. Internet-connected smart devices may sometimes provide easy ways to penetrate corporate networks, especially if default passwords (often available online) are not changed.

One problem is that these devices are often quite simple, designed for particular purposes and with little programming power that enables them to be 'intelligent' about security.

This threat to network security is a big issue. It is already recognised by the IT industry although the nature of some current Internet of Things (IoT) devices can cause problems. As a result it is necessary to audit any smart devices within an organisation to see whether default passwords have been changed and to identify (and if necessary restrict) the access they have to wider corporate networks.

PHYSICAL SECURITY

However, the threats from the Internet of Things go beyond network security.

For instance, if the security camera's data is accessed by unauthorised people then this is a threat in itself. There are already instances of baby monitors being hacked so why not an office or shop security camera?

Case Study: Hacking a Baby Monitor

In April 2014 a mother in Ohio was woken by a voice coming from her 10-month-old baby's bedroom. The mysterious voice was saying 'Wake up baby. Wake up baby'. The child's father rushed into the room and was surprised to see the baby monitor turn to face him. The voice started screaming obscenities. Naturally enough the father unplugged the camera.

In this case there was no real danger to the family although of course they felt very disturbed. But unauthorised access to a security camera in a corporate environment could potentially have security implications.

What are the dangers here? At its simplest, being able to access a security camera could mean being able to switch it off, point it in an unwanted direction or destroy video records: all these have obvious physical security issues.

There are other dangers too. Security cameras remotely operated by criminals or hacktivists might pick up the details of confidential documents. Lighting and heating could be switched off remotely to cause business disruptions. Factory machinery could be compromised as happened in December 2014 when a sophisticated spear-phishing attack at a German steelworks enabled hackers to get access to the office network and from there to the production networks. The malicious code the hackers inserted disrupted control system components that led to a blast furnace not being able to be turned off in the required way. The result was massive damage to the system.

While cyber-physical attacks, where malicious software is used to cause physical damage, are rare, they are not unknown. The Stuxnet worm used to damage Iranian uranium enrichment machinery in 2010 was an early example. And some observers believe that an oil pipeline explosion in Turkey in 2008 was caused by hackers disabling alarms and increasing the pressure in the pipeline.

DATA SECURITY

There may be other risks. Combine camera data with facial recognition software and images on Facebook and you have in theory a way of identifying shoppers. If that data got into the public domain you have a theoretical breach of data protection laws. That's not likely of course. But what happens if I am not interested in shoppers, but I am interested in a few high-profile individuals? Potentially it would be possible to get the images of senior people in a particular industry and then see who is visiting which suppliers or clients. That could be very valuable strategic information.

Alternatively (and perhaps more feasible) security camera data could be used in phishing and pharming scams. Find out when and where members of a company go for lunch, send them emails saying they are due a free loyalty sandwich because they visited at a certain time, ask them to register their details, and take them to a site that downloads keylogging software ...

Of course you could do this without accessing the security camera data if you wanted. But the beauty (if that's the right word) of hacking an Internet of Things device is that you don't have to be present and you can therefore target numerous organisations from the comfort of your own bedroom.

So far, there aren't too many examples of remote hacking of Internet-connected devices, although smart refrigerators have been implicated in at least one cyber attack on a website. But give it time.

Senior managers should ask themselves, and their IT teams, how secure the organisation's smart devices are? Starting with an audit of how many such devices are operated by the organisation is an excellent start.

PART III

Managing Cyber Risk

(14) Developing a Cyber Security Strategy

Cyber risks can cause damage to many parts of an organisation – reputations can be damaged, efficiency can be reduced, employee well-being can be compromised, strategic information can be leaked, and sales can be lost. Sometimes this damage is a result of malicious or mischievous people; sometimes it is simply a result of ignorance or carelessness.

Managers need to understand this and to ensure that appropriate strategies are in place to provide a structure for managing and mitigating cyber risk. Importantly these strategies need to accept that cyber risk isn't simply confined to computing equipment owned by the organisation. Managing cyber security is not simply a tactic of the IT department. It is a strategic organisational imperative that literally everyone in the organisation needs to be involved with, from the chief exec to the newest intern in the post room. It is a strategy that needs to be well led, agile, pragmatic and to go beyond IT networks and into every corner of the organisation.

STRATEGIC PRINCIPLES

To be effective, cyber security strategies need to be:

- holistic: involving all elements of an organisation, not just the computer network;

- appropriate: defining where the most effort needs to be spent to defend against risks and where risks are acceptable;

- led effectively: sponsored by senior people who have a view of the whole business and not just one function;

- agile: constantly being revisited and updated in the face of a rapidly changing technological environment;

- engaging: communicated to the whole organisation in such a way that everyone accepts their responsibility to be part of the cyber security solution.

A HOLISTIC APPROACH

A cyber security strategy needs to look beyond the corporate information network and corporate equipment such as desktop computers.

It should accept that employees' private devices may be used to store, access and manipulate corporate data. It should review the risks presented by use of networks other than corporate networks, for instance social media, project-management tools like Basecamp, or document-sharing tools like Google Docs and Dropbox. And it should address the risks created by the devices, networks and policies of third parties such as suppliers who have access (or could potentially have access) to your networks.

APPROPRIATE

An important element of any cyber security strategy will be to decide what information most needs to be protected. For most organisations it will be impossible, or at least unnecessarily burdensome, to protect all corporate information.

And there is always a trade-off between security and convenience: go too far in the direction of security (especially without explaining why this is necessary) and colleagues are likely to look for ways of working around security requirements in order to enhance their own convenience. A key process is therefore to prioritise the importance of information through a process of 'data classification'.

Data classification can have several purposes, for instance making data easier to retrieve or helping to ensure data is not duplicated. But it also has an important role in cyber security because data should be classified according to its importance and thus its security and encryption level.

For instance an organisation might have four levels of data importance:

● *Critical:* Highly sensitive data that if leaked could put employees at physical risk of harm, or put the organisation at risk from financial, legal or regulatory penalties, substantial fraud, or substantial competitive disadvantage. Examples would be customer credit card numbers, employee health records, network passwords, or new product designs.

- *Confidential:* Sensitive data that if leaked could have a negative impact on operational efficiency. Examples might include sales figures, contracts with third parties, or strategic plans.

- *Private:* Corporate data that is not intended to be public but that might cause inconvenience but would do little harm if leaked. Examples could include business process documents such as a skills matrix, competitor benchmarking reports, or internal telephone lists.

- *Public:* Corporate data that is intended for public distribution. Examples might include product specification sheets, contact details, and corporate newsletters.

Data classification will help you classify individual files in terms of how they are treated from a cyber risk perspective; for instance your organisation might identify four different ways of treating data (all of which could potentially apply to the same file):

- This data must be encrypted in all circumstances or in certain circumstances (e.g. when on a portable data store): this may apply to particularly sensitive data such as customer and employee personal details.

- This data must be tracked when taken outside the corporate network: this may apply to data that is strategically sensitive (implementing this implies investment in appropriate software and this may be beyond the resource of some organisations).

- Editing rights to this data are restricted to certain people (or to a certain process e.g. certain people may edit the data but other people need to sign it off): this is likely to apply to all data that will be made available to the public as there will always be a need for quality control.

- This data has access rights that are restricted to certain people (i.e. not everyone is allowed to see the data – for instance salary data or other personnel records would naturally be restricted to HR executives).

In addition to identifying the way different types of data need to be protected it is also useful to analyse the different types of threats your organisation may face. A small retailer is unlikely to suffer from an attack that knocks over their ecommerce website but might well experience a ransomware attack. A small manufacturer of high-tech equipment might experience an attempt to hack into their information network. A large organisation operating in a controversial area such as fossil fuels or GE crops might well experience an attack designed to take down their website or an attempt to hijack their social media pages. You cannot always protect against everything, and if you cannot then identifying the most likely threats (perhaps those already experienced by similar organisations) is a good starting point.

THE ROLE OF LEADERSHIP

The involvement of organisational leadership is essential if cyber risk is to be managed effectively. It is not just that risk management is part of corporate governance. It is because the attitude of leaders will affect how seriously people throughout an organisation take cyber security.

The primary responsibility for cyber risk management belongs to managers within an organisation. However, directors are responsible for ensuring that managers have implemented and are maintaining effective cyber risk management processes. These processes need to include:

● Prevention: how to protect the organisation from a damaging cyber event (not just cyber attacks by third parties).

● Response: how to respond when a damaging cyber event happens.

Directors need sufficient knowledge to quiz managers about these cyber risk management processes and to evaluate them.

AGILE PROCESSES

The cyber risk landscape is constantly evolving. Most organisations will need to rely on specialists to ensure that technical cyber risks are being managed, for instance through constantly updated virus checkers and fraud site databases.

However, there is also a need to ensure that internal processes are revisited on a regular basis and that any people-based risks such as an increased use of 'bring your own cloud' are also reviewed. 'Regularly' should mean at least twice a year and ideally more frequently.

ENGAGING

Everyone employed by, and connected with, an organisation should be regarded as being essential to cyber security. A cleaner who notices than employees are in the habit of leaving their computer switched on and logged in overnight has a responsibility to report this. A manager who notices that personal information is accessible in unencrypted files on the corporate network has a responsibility to report this. An intern who notices that a director is engaging in risky behaviour such as downloading files from the corporate network via public wi-fi should report this (tactfully). Anyone who notices and reports a potential cyber risk should be rewarded, at least with words of appreciation.

In order to be engaging to employees, cyber security procedures should be convenient, reasonable and credible:

- *Convenient:* Procedures should not cause people undue inconvenience. A procedure that demands a new password every week will probably be undermined by people using an easy-to-remember (and easy-to-break) password or will result in a loss of productivity or massively increased IT help-centre costs.

- *Reasonable:* Procedures should not be unreasonable or draconian. A procedure that forbids people from using Facebook at work without good reason will probably be undermined by people accessing Facebook via their personal devices or by people simply leaving for a job elsewhere

- *Credible:* Procedures should be credible – that is to say, useful for the organisation and effective. A system that prevents a user from downloading an email attachment but allows the user to forward the same email externally would not necessarily be credible. Systems and processes that are not credible tend to be ignored.

⑮ Picking the Right Team

You can't leave cyber security to one person. This isn't just because cyber threats occur across organisations, not just in the IT department. It's because a variety of skills are needed to handle different cyber threats and because many incidents will simply be too big for one person to handle adequately.

A good team will need an effective leader, a core team from across the organisation, ad hoc members who have specialist knowledge that can be called on where necessary, and contacts with any necessary external resources.

THE LEADER

A team has to start with a leader. While cyber risks vary considerably (from network hacking, through careless personal data loss, to social media reputation damage) it is generally sensible to have a single person leading the cyber risk team.

This person needs to have the following personal traits:

- calm under pressure, unlikely to panic and able to delegate;

- experienced and with a good understanding of the business your organisation operates in – to take a holistic view of the business, not just the threat to a particular function such as IT or marketing;

- able to understand the very different nature of different cyber risks occurring as a result of technology failures, weak business processes or naïve and careless people;

- pragmatic and able to choose actions that are underpinned by common sense and that are achievable by the organisation.

The cyber risk leader needs to be acknowledged as the leader, to have accountability for managing risk, and also to have the 'power' to ensure that any decisions made are implemented. As a result the cyber risks leader needs to be a senior person, ideally at board level. It is pointless having two leaders with equal power, or to have a cyber risk leader whose authority is constantly undermined by a more senior person.

Because this is an important position, with skills that are constantly liable to be called on, it is necessary for the cyber risk leader to have an acknowledged deputy who will be available if the leader is not and who, in the absence of the leader, has equal power.

THE CORE TEAM

It is likely that most cyber incidents have a number of different causes. As mentioned elsewhere these causes can be categorised as technology, business process and people causes. Take a hacking attack on a network. This may appear to be a technological risk best solved by software. But there can be a 'people' element to it – perhaps someone has uploaded malware to an office computer after a phishing attack. And there could be a 'process' element to it, for instance the use of a weak password or a failure to control access to the network.

For that reason it is sensible to have a core team that includes people who understand these different types of risk, perhaps someone from the IT department, someone from HR and someone from operations. Some of these people may be unfamiliar with cyber risk management and will need appropriate training.

DEFINING ROLES

Define the roles and responsibilities of everyone in the team so that everyone is clear as to who is responsible for what during the incident management process. As well as deciding how to manage the incident, which is likely to be a team responsibility, individual roles will include:

- documentation of actions;

- communication outside the team.

SPECIALIST TEAM MEMBERS

Different incidents may require different specialists to join the risk management team:

- Network penetration will require specialist IT knowledge.

- A social media crisis will require specialist marketing and social media skills.

- A compliance problem caused by the loss of personal data may require specialist legal/compliance knowledge as well as PR support.

OUTSIDE SUPPORT

It may not always be the case that the organisation has sufficient knowledge or resource internally. Appropriate contacts with external parties should be formed and these can include:

- cyber security experts;

- law enforcement;

- public relations;

- disaster recovery.

COMMUNICATION

Responsibility may include 24-hour availability so after-hours contact information for team members, and their deputies, should be shared among the team.

As a cyber incident may involve the compromise or failure of business communication channels (such as business email) it is sensible to communicate via other channels such as personal Gmail addresses or mobile phones.

⑯ Getting Prepared

Suffering a cyber security breach is almost inevitable, whatever the size of the organisation. With even large organisations like eBay and the American NSA losing data then any company must realise the chances are that they will also suffer.

Good preparation won't stop a cyber security incident. But it will reduce its impact. A comprehensive and well-documented process will ensure that everyone know what they should be doing at all stages of a crisis. And importantly, a documented process means that you can practise your responses to an incident and test out your processes.

A FAILURE TO PREPARE

The risks of not preparing for a cyber security incident include losses or damage to efficiency that are not identified; inadequate responses leading to avoidable damage to loss of efficiency, reputation, or monetary value; and a failure to stop an attack from being repeated.

Unfortunately not all organisations have established good cyber risk management processes. There can be many reasons for this including:

- lack of management knowledge of the risks;

- lack of management buy-in to the importance of planning: a feeling that 'we will busk it if it ever happens';

- an inability to detect breaches of security (not just network breaches);

- lack of an incident-reporting process, possibly enhanced by a blame culture that dissuades people from reporting perceived risks;

- lack of knowledge of the requirements of incident management e.g. the need to work with the media in certain circumstances, or the sensitivities required when handling social media;

- risk management processes that are over-engineered procedures and that make response impossible; or processes that are under engineered procedures and that ignore certain risks.

HOW TO PREPARE

IMPLEMENT PREDICTIVE CAPABILITIES

Your organisation should be able to predict many (although not all) risk scenarios. This involves ranking potentially damaging incidents in terms of impact and likelihood.

It also involves having a system to identify when a potentially damaging event is about to happen, is happening, or has happened (cyber incidents are not always immediately obvious).

You (or your external IT support team) should be able to detect incidents quickly and diagnose their nature accurately. While some incidents (such as attempted network intrusion) may require considerable technical sophistication others may be detected through social media buzz monitoring or reports from third parties such as consumers saying your website isn't responding.

A key part of the prediction process is having the ability to decide if a damaging cyber incident is happening and, if so, what sort of response is needed. This means that a process of reporting particular events to a decision-maker (probably the cyber risk team leader) needs to be put into place so that the authorised decision-maker can make a call that an incident is happening and requires a particular response.

PLAN THE RESPONSE

Once an incident has been detected you will need to have a good idea of the mitigating actions required. Your intention should be to enable your organisation to have preparations in place that will prevent damage, limit damage, or enable a quicker recovery.

As mentioned in the previous chapter, you will need the right team to manage the incident. And they will need to know what to do: how to manage the incident effectively and in a timely manner such that damage is minimised and repair can be undertaken.

This will mean agreeing actions to be taken in certain circumstances. For instance if a DDoS attack on your website is experienced they will need to know what options they have such as hiring more bandwidth, taking the website offline, or switching to a second Internet connection for external communications. The actions you agree in advance may not be exactly appropriate when a cyber incident arrives, but they will at least mean you have a good starting point and are therefore less likely to panic or go off in the wrong direction.

To achieve this you will need to document an incident-response process that includes procedures, checklists and guidelines for different types of incident (e.g. network intrusion, loss of mobile device containing data, social media crisis).

In particular you may need to consider:

- Escalation process so that the most serious breaches are handled at an appropriate level.

- Identification of situations where the support of specialists will be necessary (e.g. lawyers, public relations, forensic penetration testing, network security specialists).

- Identification of situations that need to involve law enforcement or regulatory authorities.

- A method of documenting the incident, and its effects, as it happens.

- Creation of communication plans (to customers, employees, shareholders, regulators, suppliers, the media), including the drafting of holding statements that can be adapted and made public to explain what is happening and what you are doing about it.

TEST YOUR PLANS

Once plans have been written they should be tested. Methods can include:

- Testing the awareness and skills of people in the organisation, particularly against phishing but also against physical 'incursions' such as an unauthorised man in a white coat strolling into a building.

- Testing whether security software is robust, using manual 'penetration testing' techniques if resources permit.

- Reviewing the degree to which existing systems are successful in detecting and defeating any attacks and the extent to which false positives and false negatives are delivered.

In addition you should practise your response to a cyber incident. It is all very well having a plan. But reacting to a cyber incident can be very stressful. Simulating a crisis, to give people a taste of what a cyber incident might actually be like, can be valuable. A number of companies have developed 'games' that simulate a cyber attack or a social media crisis.

These simulations are not cheap but are worth considering if you can afford them. They have the benefit of exposing people to the stress of rapid decision-making made on the basis of uncertain, and possibly contradictory, evidence. And they have the very considerable advantage of stress-testing the plans you have put in place to manage cyber incidents.

MAKE PLANS FOR AFTER THE INCIDENT

Even the worst cyber incidents don't last for ever. Therefore, a plan for what to do after an incident is very helpful. If you don't have a plan then important information that could help you manage a future incident may be lost.

Plans for after a significant cyber incident that you could develop include:

- a method of matching the incident to any predicted risks and causes in order to identify improvements to risk management processes that will prevent or limit recurrence;

- processes for repairing any damage (including making insurance claims if appropriate) and addressing any newly discovered vulnerabilities;

- disaster recovery plans in the event of a serious incident such as the destruction, corruption or leakage of key files.

(17) Developing a Risk Register

An essential part of your security plans should be to develop a register of cyber risks. Cyber risks are no different from other risks. Some are easy to predict while others are largely hidden. Identifying as many risks as possible is important and a combination of imagination and historical analysis is needed. Not all risks have the same importance: some are unlikely but would have a major impact if they happened; others are predictable but less damaging. Identifying the relative importance of each risk and then agreeing appropriate mitigating measures is a fundamental part of cyber security.

IDENTIFYING RISKS

It's not always easy to spot where cyber risks may exist. However, identifying how potential problems can occur is vital if an organisation is to create plans for managing cyber risks. There are a number of techniques that you can use to identify possible problems:

- Develop 'what if' scenarios: identify some unwanted events such as network penetration and work back to see how these events might occur.

- Identify cyber breaches that have happened to your organisation, competitors and organisations in other industries in the past.

- Ask colleagues and other stakeholders such as clients and suppliers about the cyber security issues that keep them awake at night.

- Identify critical information in your organisation and then conduct interviews with the information 'owners' to identify ways it might be compromised or leaked.

IDENTIFYING UNKNOWN RISKS

Because of the rapidly moving nature of digital technology, unknown risks and extreme unexpected events ('Black Swans') are an ever-present, and increasing, danger. Managing risks that you don't know about is difficult but strategies for doing this are emerging. These include:

- Crisis assumption: assuming that critical incidents will happen regularly and therefore acting to protect critical infrastructure and build in buffers e.g. assuming that someone will break in to the network with intent to steal and therefore planning to reduce the impact by encrypting data, creating internal firewalls, providing fake data 'baits', implementing persistent tracking on data, or even taking systems offline.

- Brains trust: creating a team of people from across the organisations (not just security specialists) whose role is to identify potential existential crises (such as total data destruction) and 'free think' defences and responses by questioning technical and other assumptions.

MANAGING THE IMPACT OF RISKS

The next step is to identify the likely effect of each risk. If you can understand the likely effect then you can identify the best ways of reducing its effect. This is likely to be a combination of techniques to:

- reduce the likelihood of its occurrence;

- reduce the impact of the event;

- recover from the event.

In order to understand each risk you have identified you will need to ask some questions such as:

- What is the nature of the risk? Is it a compliance issue? Is it a threat to our competitiveness from data leakage or data loss? Is the threat to operational efficiency, revenue or reputation?

- How acute is the risk? Can we accept it or do we need to prevent it completely, perhaps by stopping a particular activity?

- Where can we best manage the risk? Should we address people's behaviour, our business processes, or the security systems we have in place?

Once you have analysed each risk, you can then start to identify ways of mitigating them:

1. First of all, make sure that you understand the nature of the system at risk. What is the nature of the information or system and how important is it to your organisation (and what level of risk would the organisation find acceptable)? Who has access to it? At what points do people have access to the information: are these points properly secured?

2. Next, identify likely threats. Who else might want to gain access to the information or system? Why would they want to? (Reasons could be monetary gain, maliciousness, or strategic advantage.) What else might cause a problem: for instance, environmental factors, issues with suppliers, regulatory change?

3. Once you have identified the threats, evaluate each one against the vulnerability of the system as it is at the moment. Is the system as secure as it could be against each threat? Would current controls identify potential events as they arise and would they protect against them adequately? What is the likelihood of damage occurring? And what would the cost of this damage be?

4. Finally, identify and select additional security controls to eliminate the risks or lower them to an acceptable level. You will need to decide whether the cost of these additional actions is reasonable (compared with the potential loss). You will also need to ensure that your

tactics and reasons are shared with senior management so that they can re-evaluate the level of risk they are prepared to bear with each threat.

QUANTIFYING CYBER RISKS

Once you have identified as many risks as possible, the next step is to quantify each risk that you have identified in terms of:

● probability of the event

● impact of the event on the organisation

There is no one correct way of quantifying cyber risks but you could consider a 3- or 5-level scale along the following lines.

First of all consider probability:

Level	%	Definition	Indicator: In the last 3 years	Score
Very low	0–5	Extremely unlikely or impossible	Things that would cause this have not occurred	1
Low	6–15	Low but not impossible	Things that would cause this have almost happened	2
Medium	16–50	Could well occur	Things that would cause this have occurred once or twice	3
High	51–85	More likely to occur than not	Things that would cause this have occurred several times	4
Very high	86–100	Will almost certainly will occur	Things that would cause this occur frequently, say every month	5

There are some questions you can ask to help with estimating probability such as:

- How often have these or similar incidents happened in the past and to what extent have we fixed the cause of these incidents?

- Have we got any data that might throw light on these risks (e.g. the number of attempted penetrations each month) and is this data reliable and enough to analyse statistically?

It's easy to get spooked by cyber risk. But not every incident would be a disaster. And not every risk is likely. It helps to identify the nature of the threats you face. For instance:

- Theft of client data: this is more likely to happen if our organisation is trading with people on line than if it is merely providing them with product information.

- Theft of money: this is more likely to happen if we are a very cash-rich organisation rather than one with little money in the bank.

- Theft of IP and strategic data: if the IP we hold is significant and could be profitably used by other organisations then this information will be at risk and needs protection.

- Embargoed information: temporarily secret information such as the annual report before it is published is more likely to be at risk in the days before publication than in the weeks before (when it will still be in draft) or the days after.

Next consider impact. One way of identifying the likely impact of cyber risks is to try to identify how much they will cost your organisation. To help with this you can ask how much did these incidents cost us last time round and how accurate was our estimate of the costs of the previous incidents?

When estimating the cost of a potential cyber incident, you should consider three types of cost:

1. The damage that the incident will do to your organisation.

2. The cost of fixing the damage.

3. The cost of preventing future incidents.

Once you have decided on a way of rating the impact of the potential incidents you can score each risk just as you did for likelihood. I have used a scale of 1 to 20 here but it could just as easily be 1 to 5, or anything you choose:

Very low	Minor impact in one or two areas of organisation	2
Low	Minor impact across many areas of organisation	4
Medium	Medium impact across one or two areas of organisation	8
High	Medium impact across many areas of organisation	12
Very high	Major impact across one or two areas of organisation	16
Critical	Major impact across many areas of organisation	20

Now multiply the two scores (likelihood and impact) together. Thus a *Very high probability/High impact* event would have a score of 5 × 12 = 60, while a *Low probability/Medium impact* event would have a score of 2 × 8 = 16.

You must then decide how you are going to react to risks depending on how they score. For instance, you might decide that:

- risks between 80 and 100 should be terminated (i.e. any activity that could cause them should cease);

- risks between 32 and 64 should be mitigated as a priority;

- risks between 16 and 32 should be mitigated as soon as possible;

- risks between 2 and 12 can be tolerated and reacted to when necessary.

You may choose to give additional weight to 'existential' risks (i.e. risks that could result in the dissolution of your organisation) even if they are low risk.

DOCUMENTING RISKS

Once you have identified the risks your organisation is subject to and have evaluated and prioritised them it is essential to document them in a risk register.

Depending on your organisation you may already have a risk register. But if you don't then setting one up to manage cyber risks is helpful.

Individual risks can be documented in many ways. An example is shown below:

TEMPLATE FOR DESCRIBING A CYBER RISK

Risk name: Trumpton Widgets Twitter feed hacked
Risk owner: Marketing Director
Date risk registered or updated: 01.06.2015

Description	Company Twitter feed is taken over by hackers and brand credibility is then affected by inappropriate content being posted
Cause	Disaffected customers, Hacktivism
Possible catalytic events	Ineffective customer service incidents; problems with product quality; widget industry as a whole is criticised in the media
Result	Loss of control of Twitter feed
Nature of impact	Potential for lost sales costing upwards of £1 million
Stakeholders	Sales, Finance, PR
Current mitigations	Social media policy; Social media team training; Password protocol
Assurance control	Regular review by IT
Trend and trend factors	Upwards due to increased consumer activism and increasing use of Twitter
Potential factors that could change score	Company develops a CRM programme based around Twitter making Twitter even more important to our business
Status with existing mitigations	Probability 2 Impact 16 Score 32
Approach to risk	~~Accept, Transfer~~, Reduce, ~~Avoid~~
Requirement	Further mitigation to be discussed at cyber risk team meeting on 10.6.2015

In this particular case the decision in the risk register has been made that the risk is sufficiently important to require further mitigation and the cyber risk team will discuss this at their next meeting. Possible actions could be to strengthen the password protocol and to employ two-factor authentication when people sign on to Twitter or use single sign on software.

⑱ Managing the Impact of Cyber Incidents

A corporate risk management expert will tell you that there are four main ways of managing risks:

1. Avoid them: Remove the risk through the elimination of the activity or situation that presents the risk.

2. Transfer them: Load the risk onto a third party through insurance, leasing equipment, or contract wording.

3. Reduce them: Minimise the likelihood or impact of the incident through training, processes, resources, etc.

4. Retain them: Accept that some risks are inevitable or not cost-effective to manage.

Cyber risk management is no different although the precise actions you can take will depend on the individual risks.

AVOID CYBER RISK

Some cyber risks are possible to avoid. For instance the risk of strategic data leaking from a personal smartphone that gets lost is avoidable if you forbid people to bring smartphones into an office environment or connect them to corporate systems. Some particularly risk-averse organisations do this, although there is a downside to this strategy in terms of a loss of employee-work flexibility and potentially a negative effect on morale, especially with younger workers.

Some ways of avoiding a breach of cyber security include:

- A ban on taking smartphones into offices: this prevents them being used to film or photograph secret information. The downside is that this will cause irritation to your workforce.

- A ban on connecting personal devices to corporate networks: this prevents corporate data being stored on personal devices and subsequently leaking if the device is lost. The downside is that this can reduce flexibility of working and hence productivity.

- A requirement that any files uploaded to corporate laptops are encrypted prior to upload: this prevents data leakage if laptops are lost. The downside is that decrypting every single file, including ones that are not secret, will cause irritation to employees.

- A ban on the use of social media sites at work: this prevents a loss of employee productivity. The downside is that it is likely to result in lower morale and in any case people are likely to work around it by using personal smartphones to access social media sites.

Note that these solutions all come with fairly major downsides. Note also that a policy that attempts to avoid a risk may merely disguise it. Take the risk of information leaking out. A ban on downloading a particular file to an external device or attaching it to an email could potentially be worked around by an employee taking a screen grab, cutting and pasting data from the file, taking a photograph, or simply taking hand-written notes.

Methods of avoiding cyber risk may be appropriate for some highly secure organisations (such as certain government services and high-tech industries). But for many organisations the downsides will outweigh the benefits. And sometimes, you simply have to trust people!

TRANSFER CYBER RISK

Some cyber risks are transferrable. There is a growing market for cyber risk insurance for instance. Most of this protection refers to monetary loss caused by network attacks. However, some risks are uninsurable because the potential costs are impossible to evaluate; these include reputation damage, loss of trust from stakeholders such as regulators, and lowered employee morale.

INSURING AGAINST CYBER RISKS

One strategy for managing risk is to transfer it to another party. And one way of doing that is to buy insurance. While not all cyber risk is insurable, a good deal is and today there are dozens of companies offering cover. Coverage can include protection against:

- Costs arising from information leakage such as a failure to keep corporate, personal or third-party information private; losses here can include legal costs (defending actions by regulators and by people affected by the data leakage), PR costs, the cost of notifying people affected by the loss (such as consumers whose personal data has been stolen), and fines.

- Costs arising from a failure of third-party associates to keep information private.

- Costs arising from third parties who claim damage as a result of the security breach, for instance because of virus transmission.

- Costs arising from business interruption caused by a security failure (e.g. inability to access files or to continue with e-commerce trading).

- The costs of any payments to blackmailers who are threatening data destruction.

- The cost of repairing damage caused by hackers, 'forensic' work to detect the cause of the damage, work to avoid any future repeats of the incident, and the costs of data recovery after a security breach.

USING THIRD-PARTY SERVICES

The use of third parties such as online payment processors or specialist companies with certified and audited capabilities in cyber security (under strictly defined service level agreements with appropriate compensation clauses), can also potentially transfer at least some risk to the specialist organisation, for instance allowing an organisation to escape regulatory censure.

Note, though, that while your organisation might escape a fine from a regulator, consumers are likely to be less forgiving and will blame your organisation for losing their data, irrespective of whose fault it really is.

REDUCE CYBER RISK

There are many ways of reducing cyber risk. The creation of a detailed risk register (see Chapter 17) will have enabled you to identify the most obvious risks. Once you have identified them you may be able to take cost-effective steps to reduce their impact or likelihood.

It is pointless to outline all the steps that can be taken to reduce cyber risk in a book of this nature, but as a flavour here are some tips for reducing particularly significant cyber risks:

- Back up: Back up important data on a monthly basis and test the backups to ensure they can be read.

- Encrypt: Always encrypt sensitive data, especially when transferring by wi-fi or storing on portable devices such as mobile phones and memory sticks.

- Ensure data is securely destroyed: Ensure files are properly destroyed and not simply deleted; eliminate unnecessary copies of backup data; dispose of devices only after they have been wiped clean of data.

- Reduce the effect of incursions: separate computers that handle critical information (e.g. customer credit card details) from computers handling routine information (e.g. email).

- Strengthen passwords: Change default passwords; insist on adequate passwords that are different for different applications and that are changed regularly; opt for two-factor authentication whenever possible.

- Restrict access: Allow employees access only to information that is necessary for their tasks; restrict what they can do with information (e.g. read, edit and read, share, edit and read); ensure employees have to log on to access information; old user accounts should be deleted at the time of departure and passwords changed as appropriate.

- Limit activity: Put limits on what anyone can do in a single session. It should not, for instance, be possible to copy all the data on the corporate network in one go or to transfer funds above a certain amount in a single session.

- Update software: Ensure software such as firewalls, browsers and VPNs are regularly updated; delete unused software or store it outside the system.

- Office security: Ensure that access to work premises and to any computing equipment is strictly regulated; do not allow visitors and temporary staff to wander around freely unless you are totally certain they are not a threat.

- Train: Educate employees to use common sense and follow guidelines about cyber security and social media, especially about the risks of phishing and malware; publish formal policies on information security, Bring Your Own Device, Bring Your Own Cloud, and social media use and make sure employees understand these (and sanctions for not following them).

- Wi-fi: Avoid public wi-fi if at all possible; if it is necessary to use public wi-fi, employ a VPN and avoid sensitive activities such as banking or logging on to a corporate network.

The UK government has published a number of helpful papers on cyber security for small and large organisations. These are worth consulting, although they don't necessarily cover all the cyber risks organisations are faced with. Start with:

- *Cyber Essentials* (www.cyberstreetwise.com/cyberessentials/)

- *10 steps to Cyber Security* (https://www.gov.uk/government/ publications/cyber-risk-management-a-board-level-responsibility/10-steps-summary)

- *Cyber Security: balancing risk and reward with confidence: Guidance for Non-Executive Directors* (https://www.gov.uk/ government/uploads/system/uploads/attachment_data/ file/385009/bis-14-1277-cyber-security-balancing-risk-and-reward-with-confidence-guidance-for-non-executive-directors.pdf)

In addition The Institute of Risk Management published a very helpful document on cyber risk management in 2014; the full document is only available to members but a detailed summary is available to anyone online (https://www.theirm. org/knowledge-and-resources/thought-leadership/cyber-risk/).

RETAIN CYBER RISK

In some cases it will be appropriate to retain certain cyber risks. It is impossible to guard against cyber risk totally and while some cyber risk can be reduced or transferred, doing this for all cyber risk may not be cost-effective or may be simply too expensive for some organisations. Thus single sign-on systems, data tracking systems and mobile device management systems may be too expensive for smaller organisations to afford.

Similarly the use of personal devices or personal email at work may well be accepted as a security risk (employees may use them to steal corporate information) because the cost of managing these risks is too high in terms of damage to employee morale or productivity. In this case the only option is to accept the risk.

⑲ Responding to Incidents

Suffering from a damaging cyber security incident doesn't have to be the end of the world. As you will know if you have done your planning, there is a structured way of responding to incidents that will help you make the right decisions and employ the right resources.

DETECTING AND VERIFYING

The first stage is (obviously) to detect an incident. This could happen automatically if it is a network attack that is identified by network security protocol. Or your company may subscribe to a 'threat intelligence' service that provides information about potential attacks. Alternatively it could be an individual employee reporting something such as a phishing attack that may have led to malware upload. Or it could be a physical security breach or some risky behaviour being observed.

Many incidents are spotted by people outside an organisation and it is important for organisations to make it easy for people to report these incidents as well as having a culture that takes these reports seriously.

An important part of the 'detecting' stage is verification that an apparent attack is a real attack. 'False positives' (when threat monitoring systems highlight incidents that don't actually exist) can be as dangerous as a failure to detect an attack as too many false positives can result in the monitoring system simply being ignored.

THREAT INTELLIGENCE

Many large organisations, especially those in high-risk areas such as financial services, employ threat intelligence services. Threat intelligence is designed to identify potential threats before they happen. The services undertake a number of different activities that may include lurking in 'dark net' chat rooms to pick up on significant conversations, monitoring the purchase of malware or the trading of credit card details on the dark net, gathering intelligence from across an industry on new phishing attacks, or monitoring the purchase of 'look alike' URLs that may be used for fraud (for instance Bungle Bank may have registered Bungle.com as its main address and find that apparent fraudsters are registering 1Bungle.com, Bung1e.com and Bungle.co as sites that could be used to defraud people). These services are not cheap and will generally be outside the budget of small and medium-sized organisations.

One of the problems with threat intelligence service is the 'Fire-hose' effect: too much data to make sense of. Large companies especially may see many potential threats every hour. It can be hard to detect what is a real threat and what isn't. Some people think that the reason US retailer Target failed to respond to the threat intelligence it received was simply because they had so many apparent threats that they ignored the real ones.

It is important to treat threat intelligence carefully as damaging 'false positives' are always possible. Take this real-life example. An e-commerce company experienced a tenfold rise in traffic to their website. At first sight this appeared to be the initial build-up of a Denial of Service attack designed to take the website down.

The company felt that the right approach was to take their website down temporarily so that the attackers would go elsewhere. However, the security consultant they employed did some basic investigation, asking people across the company whether there might be a reason for the increase in traffic. There was: a new TV advertisement about their website, encouraging people to visit it for special offers, had just aired. Taking the website down would have meant a big revenue loss and a wasted investment in marketing.

Because of the fire-hose effect and the danger of false positives, an important question to ask IT professionals is, 'Are you confident that the systems you have in place will allow you to identify significant threats promptly and accurately?'

REPORTING AND ASSESSING

Once an incident (or potential incident) has been spotted, a report needs to be made to a person with authority to manage the incident. This requires certain internal processes to be set up such as appointing and publicising the person or people who should receive reports, as well as educating all staff in the nature of cyber risks and how to reduce them.

People who receive incident reports need then to decide whether there is an incident in progress and, if there is, the importance of the incident and thus how it will be handled. Incidents can be classified on a scale of intensity, as for instance:

- critical (attacks that are hard to contain or recover from; incidents that could put someone at risk of physical harm; incidents that might upset large numbers of customers or that could cause substantial reputational damage; events that are at risk of being picked up by media or regulators);

- harmful (attacks or breaches of process that can be contained relatively easily; incidents that will only affect a few people);

- trivial (incidents that don't necessarily need immediate action but which should be monitored and which may point to larger risks elsewhere).

- In addition some threats may be categorised as long-term persistent threats, possibly caused by ingrained behaviour, that need a long-term strategy.

The process of assessing and reporting an incident is important: if too many incidents deemed dangerous turn out to be trivial, or if senior management are informed about every little incident, then the wider management team may start to discount the warnings they are receiving and fail to act when a really dangerous incident occurs. It is important to remember that not everything is an emergency!

THREAT LEVELS AND THE KILL CHAIN

A potentially damaging cyber event such as network penetration can be handled in different ways depending on how immediate it is. The analysis of how immediate a threat is sometimes uses a 'kill chain'. This involves dividing the threat into a series of stages such as:

1. Reconnaissance: the target is being picked; threat intelligence may identify if you are at risk and if so in what way (for instance, is your customer database at risk by criminals or are hackers trying to take you offline completely for political purposes?)

2. Weaponisation: the attack is made ready, for instance off-the-shelf malware is bought.

3. Delivery: the initial attack happens, for instance a phishing email is sent out and opened by the target.

4. Exploitation: the code that has been delivered by the phishing email runs on the victim's computer.

5. Installation: the hacker uses the vulnerability created by the code to download the tools they need to achieve what they want.

6. Action: the hacker uses the downloaded tools to achieve their wicked ends – for instance the uploading of the victim's database of clients.

Depending on the stage within the kill chain, there may be different options open to the victim. For instance if stage 4 or 5 was achieved then there may be time to take defensive action such as removing the customer database or going offline but if stage 6 has been reached then there will be a need for rapid communication with affected customers as well as regulators.

In addition the physical elements of the corporate network that has been compromised also opens up alternatives. Let's take the example of an organisation with three 'servers' (computers or parts of computers that hold information or run certain programs). They have a 'staging server' used for developing website assets; this is connected to the main corporate server which holds all the key corporate information; the main server is in turn connected to a payment server that handles the customer credit cards.

If the hacker penetrates the staging server then it may be possible to isolate the attack by cutting links between the staging server and the main corporate server without a big risk of the payments server being compromised.

However, if the hacker penetrates the corporate server then the risk to the 'next door' payment server may be too great to allow for an attempt at isolation: the decision might be taken to close down the payment server in order to protect customers and preserve the reputation of the company at the expense of lost sales.

RESPONDING

The process of responding to an incident has two stages: containment which is designed to contain any danger in order to give the organisation time to react in order to limit damage; and then elimination of the threat.

If an incident is deemed to require a response the cyber risk team should be called into action. Their role is to contain any damage and recover any data lost or repair any systems that have been damaged.

They also need to be aware of the potential for other incidents as the initial incident may be a distraction designed to weaken the organisation prior to the main attack.

Incident management teams should understand the conditions under which law enforcement or regulators should be contacted.

The team can make it easier to decide what actions are appropriate by asking the following questions:

- What happened? When and where did it happen? To whom did it happen?

- How did it happen? What were the main causes? Were these expected?

- What is the result of the incident? How much damage has been caused? How much more damage could be caused? Who has suffered?

- Could the damage be escalated in some way? How might that happen?

- What has been done to reduce damage so far? If third parties such as customers or the general public were affected what has been done to help them?

- Who has been notified so far? What reactions have we had from them?

Once these questions have been answered the risk management team can discuss and decide on the next actions that need to be taken.

COMMUNICATING

Throughout an incident (when it arises, during its management and once it has been closed off) there will be a need to communicate with a variety of people including:

- the board, relevant specialists within the organisation and employees;

- external stakeholders such as regulators, clients, the media and customers;

- the general public.

It will be especially important to communicate with people who have been negatively affected by the security breach including customers. Ideally holding statements and template responses will have been created during the planning phase but these should be reviewed before they are used for real.

LEARNING FROM EXPERIENCE

A cyber security incident that has been successfully managed isn't over when it's over. There will still be important communication to be made to reassure customers and other stakeholders. There will be remedial action to be taken to repair any damage and strengthen existing processes. And there will be a lot of useful learning about what happened:

how did the incident arise, how was it handled, how was any damage cleared up – and what could have been done better?

DOCUMENTING AND REVIEWING

As the incident progresses it is necessary to document all actions taken and their costs (especially if an insurance claim will be made).

A log book for the incident will enable key events to be reviewed as the incident progresses. The rationale for decisions should be recorded as this could be valuable to review using hindsight.

This documentation should be reviewed at a wash-up meeting after the incident has been closed off. The intention of this very important meeting is twofold:

1. To identify how a similar incident could be prevented in the future.

2. To agree ways that a similar incident could be handled better in future.

CONTINUING COMMUNICATION

Notify any affected customers that the incident is over, ensuring that your information is accurate and sympathetic. You may also be able to advise them about what part they can play in reducing their risks in future. Take extra care to respond to customer complaints and feedback.

Continue with any public relations and social media activities, including monitoring social media for mentions of the incident.

Ensure all relevant regulatory authorities (especially data protection regulators such as the Information Commissioner and any relevant industry regulators are informed of the incident and how it was resolved.

RECOVERING FROM DAMAGE

After an incident has been avoided or successfully managed there may be actions the organisation still needs to take. These may include:

- Ensuring that any residual danger is closed off, for instance that passwords have been changed, software has been updated or network security protocols strengthened.

- Reinstating any data that has been lost or damaged; if appropriate (e.g. if data has been reinstated from a backup copy that is a few days' old) ensuring that people are aware that it may not be the most up-to-date version of the data.

- If insurance is available, preparing a report of damage and costs to date; liaising with the insurance company so they are aware of future actions to be taken in order to prevent a repeat incident.

- Liaising with law enforcement if necessary.

- Liaising with relevant security industry providers (e.g. the company providing your firewall) so that information about the breach can be shared and future versions of security tools and processes improved.

ITERATING RESPONSES

After any significant incident it is sensible to have a 'wash-up' meeting to review the way the crisis was managed and to identify potential improvements to processes and techniques.

With major incidents it is sensible to include some outsiders who can question the team and prevent self-justifying post-rationalisation.

The review should cover the following:

- Identify the main causes of the incident and whether they were foreseen.

- Compare the actual nature and intensity of the incident with the description of any risk that was identified and documented in the risk register.

- Examine the effectiveness of the risk monitoring process; consider whether other useful early warning indicators can be identified.

- Examine how effective the planned mitigation actions were; generate ideas to improve processes for handling an incident.

- Examine the effectiveness of the team and the team leadership, and the behaviour of other employees during the incident.

- Generate ideas to prevent reoccurrence or occurrence of a similar incident elsewhere.

- Consider whether the incident offers new insights into the effectiveness of the cyber security framework in place such as newly discovered weaknesses and the effectiveness of security controls.

Any revised processes should be reviewed after 12 months (or sooner) to ensure that they are working as anticipated and to give assurance that the incident has a reduced likelihood of re-occurring.

(20) Digital Governance

WHAT IS DIGITAL GOVERNANCE?

Does your organisation have sound digital governance? It might not sound like the most exciting of questions. But it is an increasingly important one.

You may not even have contemplated 'Digital governance' or come across it as a concept. So what is it? Digital governance involves the policies, processes, roles and responsibilities, guidelines, overseen by an organisation's board, that define the ways that the business opportunities and risks associated with digital technologies (including digital asset management, e-commerce, digital information systems and digital business operations) are guided and controlled.

Some people define it as 'best practice' in e-commerce, content management, digital marketing and digital asset management. But it is a lot more than that. It's about responding to, and managing the use of, digital technologies across the whole of an organisation: in finance, HR, marketing, sales, IT and operations.

Cyber security is a central part of digital governance. It's not the only part. But as your security processes may impact on other elements of cyber governance it's worth discussing here.

WHY IS DIGITAL GOVERNANCE IMPORTANT?

Digital governance is important as a separate and defined part of wider corporate governance for several reasons. The most important reason is that more and more business processes involve digital technology – with all the advantages and disadvantages that come with it. In addition digital technology is increasingly a vital part of the lives of people and so any organisation that deals with people needs to take account of it.

Then there are the regulators and the people who set quality standards. Most regulators are trying to come to terms with digital technology. It is clear that some are failing to do so adequately; and in other cases regulators are proposing guidelines that limit innovation or simply fail to protect consumers sufficiently. And in some cases technical quality standards were set more than a decade ago, have been little updated, and are no longer fit for purpose.

And finally there are managers. Many senior managers, especially those in their mid 40s and older, started in business before digital technology (and especially the Internet) really took a hold. Some of these, possibly disliking technology generally, have ignored the changes that digital technology is bringing to business and the lives of consumers. And now, perhaps frightened of being seen to be out of date, they continue to shy away from addressing their lack of knowledge. You probably know people like that.

These days, make a bad decision about digital technology and you may be causing real damage to your organisation. That can be damage to the organisation's reputation, to its ability to function efficiently, to its ability to comply with appropriate regulations, to its sales, its bank balance, even its share price.

AREAS OF OPPORTUNITY

Digital technology isn't just about hazards. It brings many opportunities. It is the failure to grasp these opportunities that presents a risk to organisations, simply because a business that neglects an opportunity is likely to find itself outcompeted by other businesses.

PRODUCT IMPROVEMENT AND NEW PRODUCT DEVELOPMENT

How is your organisation using digital technology to drive product innovation? This isn't the same as using computing equipment in products such as motor cars. It is about using digital technology to deliver new or better ways of serving markets.

The first thing to consider here is the degree to which your organisation uses data about consumers and markets to improve products and services. Many organisations collect, or have the potential to collect a huge amount of market information from a variety of sources (web analytics, call centres, sales data, social media). Often, rather than being used to provide better understanding of consumers or more relevant products for consumers, the data is neglected. While not all data is useful (and actively collecting useless data is a waste of resource) it is important to audit what you have. A few questions to ask:

- What data could we collect within processes that are or could be digitised?

- What data do we collect, and in what form? (Note that this is also an important question to ask for risk management purposes, especially if you are considering cyber risk insurance.)

- What data do we use, and what other data could be used?

- How well is the data being used and could it be used more effectively?

Data is very important. Although in my view it is important to use it for enlightenment and to contribute to decision making rather than using it as the sole reason for taking a decision. And of course there is always the risk that the data you use is somehow inappropriate – incomplete, corrupted or simply irrelevant.

Another issue to consider is the way that digital technology allows changes to products and business models. This is rather more complex to address.

Take the example of software. Once upon a time, to get some software you would buy the appropriate disks and load the software from the disks onto your computer. Before broadband Internet was commonplace computer disks were really the only way to distribute software.

Nowadays software is increasingly sold as a service rather than as a product. A company like Microsoft now likes to sell you access to their software with an annual licence rather than selling you physical disks. The access provided enables you to use the software online and offline and to get regular updates, as well as coming with lots of convenient tools such as email, calendar and document storage all neatly integrated.

That's a very different proposition to buying a set of disks: more profitable for Microsoft presumably, as well as being more convenient (but possibly more expensive) for many users.

Rethinking your organisation's products and services in such a way that they can take full advantage of digital technology is hard. And new ways of doing things come with their share of risks. But the rewards can be substantial.

BUSINESS OPERATIONS

Digital technology has many well-documented advantages when used within manufacturing processes. It is also starting to increase the opportunities for mass customisation (where a small number of people get the same product based on options they have chosen), and personalisation (where a single consumer gets a unique and exactly specified product). This is a major new marketing opportunity.

For instance digital printing is making direct mail marketing far more targetable and even having an impact on book printing. And there is a revolution happening in furniture manufacturing where designers can provide you with, say, the skeleton of a chair and you, the consumer, print (using your 3D printer) the seat panel to your very own bottom shape. This revolution may go even further in fashion where designers might provide you with customisable templates and the cloth that you print contains wearable computing that you can programme to deliver your own personal set of colour effects that change with your mood or location.

Customer service can also be improved through digital technology. For instance it is now common for engineers and meter readers to be equipped with tablets that allow instant access to information as well as instant input of customer data. (Of course this way of working may come with substantial risks of personal data loss and all that entails.)

Digital technology also brings perhaps less exciting but probably more profitable opportunities in supply chain management. For instance some organisations have automated supply chain management allowing just-in-time inventory restocking or real-time bidding by suppliers. Again though, integrating IT systems with third parties such as suppliers increases your cyber risk profile.

And there are opportunities in people management. Many of these are well established, if not always well implemented. For instance, intranets enable internal knowledge-sharing and project-working between people in different buildings. There are opportunities for flexible home-working. There is a potential for management processes such as certain parts of decision-making to be made more efficient or even totally automated. And there is, as an inevitable downside, an increased risk of strategic information or knowledge being leaked.

MARKETING AND SALES

Some of the biggest opportunities for business are in marketing and sales. These include:

- gathering (and using) useful customer data within digitised processes such as website analytics;

- using online marketing communications, including social media and personalised messaging;

- automating or increasing efficiency of business processes, including sales and customer service.

The examples above are commonplace. More interesting are the opportunities around automated and real-time pricing based on demand or the urgency of the sale, something that the airline industry is very familiar with but which has potential applications across many industries.

AREAS OF RISK

Understanding where digital risks lie is at the core of digital governance. The risks associated with digital technology are not just concerned with information; they are many and include:

- weak business strategy;

- leakage of strategic information;

- a failure of regulatory compliance;

- ineffective talent acquisition and human resource management;

- damage to operational efficiency;

- wasted investments.

Let's briefly take these one by one.

WEAK BUSINESS STRATEGY

How does digital technology affect business strategy? Senior executives need to ask themselves whether they understand consumer and technology trends; for instance, are they keeping up with the way that many consumers are moving away from fixed Internet access to smart mobile devices?

And there is a need to look wider than consumers. How are your competitors reacting to digital technology? Can you work with suppliers in a different way, cutting costs and timescales, through the use of digital? And how does digital technology affect the PESTLE (political, economic, social, technical, legal, environmental) landscape?

Finally, while no one can predict the future, it's as well to be aware of potentially disruptive technologies on the horizon. Don't spend too much time on this as it is easy to get wrong. For instance the jury is still very much out on whether wearables (at least as currently developed) will have popular applications wider than health and fitness. So spending a lot of time and effort to be a leader in this space may be wasted. Sometimes there is a lot to be said for 'second mover advantage' as Google, Apple and Facebook have all discovered.

LEAKAGE OF STRATEGIC INFORMATION

A lot of organisations fear the leakage of strategic information and build their information security processes around this, designing protection that keeps unwanted visitors out. This is of course important. But it is just as important to acknowledge that the risk may not be 'people getting in' but 'information getting out'.

Important information can get out in a variety of ways, without a hacker ever being involved. Have you left tags on your website that allow an agency you once employed access to your web analytics? Or perhaps you are using a cloud computing service like Dropbox that ex-clients or companies you have previously partnered with still have access to. Has your failure to change passwords given an opportunity to ex-employees to access corporate information? Are employees able to download sensitive documents to email or USB sticks and take them out of your office network? Are you discussing topics on social media that could give your competitors valuable insights into your plans?

OPERATIONAL EFFICIENCY

Unfortunately digital technology comes with a number of threats to operational efficiency and profitability. These include:

- data loss or damage to computer systems (or even factory machinery) as a result of hacking;

- damage to online sales due to attacks on your website;

- losses incurred due to paying ransom demands from hackers who have denied you access to your computer systems;

- damage to profitability as a result of counterfeit online trading;

- contracts entered into or varied accidentally by employees using the 'informal' channels of email or social media;

- a reduction in employee efficiency due to the unmanaged use of social media while at work;

- a failure to provide protection against consumer complaints as a result of failure to archive all communications.

The issue here for boards is to realise that the risks from digital technology exist right across organisations and are not simply confined to the loss of information held on corporate IT networks.

FAILURE OF REGULATORY COMPLIANCE

The most common compliance threat is probably that of the failure to protect personal information about employees and consumers. Until 2015 the regulatory environment in Europe was less stringent that in the USA with fines being relatively low. This is changing, though, and fines of up to 5 per cent of an organisation's global turnover will soon be levied by the EU.

Again the risks are not just from hackers. The careless loss of devices that contain 'personally identifiable information' (PII) is a large risk (and something that happens frequently). Less well known is the risk that happens when PII is transferred to a third party such as a printer who is printing direct mailing pieces for you. Do you know which third parties have access to your sensitive data? Do you know how secure they are?

A relatively common risk is the failure to comply with advertising and marketing regulations, especially when using social media, which is regarded as being informal. Do you know who handles your social media communications? Are they properly trained in what is allowable and appropriate?

Another potential risk is the inappropriate sharing of financial information, for instance on social media. While this isn't a huge risk it has happened. The danger arises because in the past most people who had access to financial information had no real way of sharing it publicly: the only way of doing so was to go via formal channels such as a PR department. But now anyone with access to financial information can tweet it or post it on Facebook.

And for some organisations there are requirements around communications, including requirements for archiving, that may not be well known. For instance the Financial Conduct Authority's guidance requires that firms take 'reasonable care to make and retain adequate records'. Most people understand that to include email. But what about Twitter, Facebook, Snapchat ...?

Potentially there are also dangers around accessibility and disability discrimination: for instance if you offer a service online and are not taking reasonable steps to provide access to the disabled (such as the visually impaired) you may be breaking the law.

HUMAN RESOURCES

Digital technology can also affect how organisations attract and retain talent, an issue of major concern to many boards. Issues to consider include:

- How to use social media profiles during the recruitment process without risking accusations of discrimination from unsuccessful candidates.

- How to manage employee use of social media at work without demotivating people and without being accused of invasion of privacy by employees.

- How to ensure that an employee's use of social media does not leave an organisation open to vicarious liability if that employee does something inappropriate such as bullying a colleague online.

- How to ensure that disciplinary processes concerned with digital technology (such as disciplining someone for failing to comply with a BYOD policy) don't result in the organisation losing unfair dismissal cases.

- How to manage any damage to the 'organisation-as-an-employer' brand that can happen via social media.

- How to ensure that irresponsible or disaffected employees cannot damage the organisation's brands by unmonitored access to social media accounts.

- How to avoid the situation where key employees have to be sacked after they say inappropriate things on social media (not uncommon).

As HR department staff may be unaware of some of these issues, it is a matter for the board to ensure that they have the right knowledge and are supported by appropriate technology and advice.

INVESTMENTS

In some circumstances the returns from investments made through digital technology can be reduced. For instance:

- Expensively developed intellectual property assets can be lost or damaged as result of piracy or hacking (think about the problems Sony Pictures had in late 2014 when much of their IP was leaked online).

- Organisations can fail to gain copyright of work they have commissioned from freelances (such as software or photographs) because of poorly worded freelance contracts.

- Social media assets, such as lists of customers and brand enthusiasts, can be lost as a result of poor employment contracts.

- Inappropriate marketing investments can be made because flawed KPIs are proposed or because managers fail to understand what campaign data really means; more dangerous perhaps are marketing strategies that divert investment because of unwise assumptions about marketplaces (for example some organisations have discovered that investing in search marketing at the expense of display advertising has resulted in rising costs because the display advertising was efficient at driving people to search for their brands).

Again, it is for the board to ensure that the assumptions that underpin investment decisions are appropriate. Questions to ask here include:

- Is any spending on digital marketing appropriate and are returns being reported accurately and in a way that is relevant to the business?

- Is there an appropriate strategy for developing digital assets across the organisation so that redundant investment (such as multiple websites and social media accounts) is avoided and responsibility for individual assets is managed in a logical fashion?

And finally it is very necessary to ensure that investments are being made with the end customer in mind by asking questions such as:

- Do web and mobile assets deliver value from a user perspective, rather than simply from an organisational viewpoint?

- Do digital investments, for instance in websites and apps, assist or hinder a consistent and positive brand experience across all marketing channels and consumer touchpoints?

REPUTATIONAL DAMAGE

Digital technology also has the power to inflict direct damage on product, brand and employer-brand reputation. This damage is different from the indirect damage to reputation that can arise from compliance failures or the failure to protect websites from attack. It generally arises from badly managed social media including:

- Damage from the use of personal social media accounts by employees who are identifiable on their social media accounts as employees (or who are prominent and known to be associated with your organisation); this damage can be caused by intemperate language or controversial opinions.

- Damage from content posted on 'hijacked' social media accounts.

- Damage from inappropriate posts on organisational social media accounts made by employees in error (thinking they were posting on their personal social media accounts) or mischievously, generally when people know that their posts cannot be traced back to them individually.

These risks are perhaps less important than the loss of personal data or the leaking of strategic information. But they happen frequently, can cause damage to morale as well as corporate reputation, and are totally unnecessary.

More dangerous is the damage to corporate reputations from the use of social media by consumers who are unhappy with your organisation or its products and services. There is little that can be done to prevent this (apart of course from ensuring products and services are always first class). The significance lies in how these incidents are handled – in the preparation organisations have put in place to manage any damage from a social media reputational crisis.

QUESTIONS FOR YOUR BOARD
OF DIRECTORS

If you are serious about digital governance then you should at least ask the following questions:

- Does a specific member of the board have acknowledged responsibility for cyber risk? Does this person have sufficient knowledge to fulfil this role?

- Is cyber risk regularly discussed at board level? Do board members have sufficient knowledge of and interest in cyber risk? Are they confident of their knowledge?

- Does the board understand the organisation's 'appetite' for risk across all organisational functions (not just IT), and is this appetite considered appropriate by the board? (For instance are there 'existential' risks that are being glossed over?)

- Are there clear lines of responsibility up to board level for reporting the occurrence and management of cyber incidents? Do cyber incidents get reported to the board?

- Is there a clear management structure for cyber risk management within the organisation including a cyber risk team leader with sufficient authority and knowledge?

- Do board members understand and comply with their responsibilities to avoid cyber risks on an individual basis? Are they leading by example?

- Is the board content that appropriate resources including technology and training are available for the management of cyber risks?

- Is the board content that appropriate processes including the identification of the most significant information, the development of risk registers, and processes for managing BYOD are in place?

- Is the board confident that measures to protect against a major breach (such as leakage of all employee personal data) have been taken? Similarly is the board confident that adequate plans are in place for response to a major breach?

- Is the organisation at risk from any existential threats caused by cyber technology?

More comprehensive advice about how company boards should address cyber security is available in HM government's *Cyber security: Balancing risk and reward with confidence. Guidance for non-executive directors.*

Afterword: Looking from the Past to the Future

Cyber security has been confined to the IT department for too long. It isn't hard to understand why.

Most senior managers, typically in their 40s, 50s and 60s, cut their business teeth in the days before the widespread use of the Internet, when IT was used for payroll management, order processing and accounting. The technology behind these systems was a mystery to most people outside IT.

Later in the 1980s, PCs started to appear on the desks of ordinary office workers, used for clunky word-processing and rudimentary presentation packages. Academics conducted studies on whether information technology increased or decreased business efficiency (at least one study indicated that computers at work decreased productivity.)

The IT professional was still king and most managers had a love-hate relationship with them, happy when a package performed as it was supposed to and frustrated when something went wrong (as it frequently did).

The world changed in many ways in 1993 when Internet browsers that could display graphics meant that the Internet left the confines of universities, government agencies and a few very early adopters, and started to be accessed in homes and offices, initially across North America and northern Europe, and then far more widely. (By the end of 2016 more than half the world's population will probably have Internet access: it's expanding at around ten people per second.)

But even with widespread use of the Internet, which connected businesses in a way they hadn't been before, most managers still had little reason to be curious about the technology. After all it didn't seem to be much more than a way to exchange messages and find information. Any security requirements, such as keeping company data safe behind a firewall, were best left to the professionals. And perhaps IT professionals exacerbated this with the use of unnecessary jargon (like DDoS and Social Engineering) to disguise relatively simple concepts. Cyber security, it was felt, simply didn't concern the C Suite.

There was no excuse for this attitude. Cyber risks have been around for a while. And some of the incidents have been enormous. For instance, in 2005 a disgruntled ex-employee of AOL stole 90 million email addresses and sold them to spammers. And around the same time unauthorised code was discovered in the network of credit card payment processor that could have compromised 40 million credit card accounts.

However, the feeling that 'it couldn't happen to us' persisted. Despite warnings from the IT industry, the idea that cyber security was best left to the professionals continued to give an opt-out to senior managers who, for whatever reason (fear, ignorance, naivety?), found it convenient to ignore the threats.

Perhaps that attitude started to change in 2012 with the discovery of a massive hack that had lasted seven or eight years against several large US businesses including JC Penney and 7-Eleven. The following year saw more huge attacks, against well-known tech companies such as Adobe, Evernote and Ubisoft, as well as the hijacking of AP's Twitter account which ultimately led to a $140 billion plunge (and recovery) of US stock markets. The year 2014 started with a giant data leak at Target and finished with another giant data leak at JP Morgan (with plenty going on in between). And 2015 has seen the highly embarrassing Centcom hack, a very troubling cyber attack on a German steelworks that managed to cause physical damage, and attacks on French and US media owners, among other incidents.

All of this has meant that cyber security is now firmly on the radar of governments and business C suites – or at least many of them. And while there may still be a lack of understanding (which I hope this book will do something to address) there is at least an acknowledgement that cyber security is an important issue.

So what does the future hold? Are we getting closer to managing cyber risk? Awareness is a good start but it isn't enough. There is education to be done, across organisations, so that everyone understands the nature of cyber risk and their responsibility (and ability) to reduce it. Educating consumers is just as important, so they can act as the eyes of organisations as well as protecting themselves from cyber criminals. There are investments to be made, not just in tools and technology fixes, but also in business and communication processes. And there are protocols to create so that people understand when and how (and indeed whether) to use efficient and flexible working methods such as Bring Your Own Device and Bring Your Own Cloud.

All of this will lead to increased cyber security. We must always guard against complacency, though, against the risks caused by Donald Rumsfeld's 'unknown unknowns', the things we don't know we don't know. There will always, almost by definition, be zero day threats. It's is far too early to say we understand all the risks posed by virtual reality, wearable computing and by the Internet of Things. And as yet no one can know what the risks brain-computer interfaces and true artificial intelligence hold.

We also need to accept that legal and ethical organisations are always at a disadvantage against criminal gangs and cyber terrorists. They just need to get lucky once while security professionals need to be successful all the time. They have an infinite number of opportunities to create code that can penetrate security, while security professionals can only guess at the most obvious opportunities and defend against them. And the criminals will always be able to exploit the trusting nature (and often the laziness) of the majority of people.

Because of this we can be sure that we will never eliminate 100 per cent of cyber risk. We can also be sure that, with the right mindset, we can eliminate most of it.

Glossary

Access control	The selective restriction of access to a file, a website or a network in order to manage who can do what with that file, website or network. Access may be defined (and controlled) in various ways; for instance some people may be able to read a document, others to read and edit it, and others to read, edit and share it
Advanced Persistent Threat (APT)	A combination of hidden and continuous hacking techniques that target a specific entity such as a large company or a government organisation over a period of time, usually sponsored by a large organisation such as a government
Attack surface	The total set of the different ways that someone can attack an IT system in order to cause damage
Back door	A feature of a supposedly secure computer system that allows secret or unauthorised access, generally for nefarious purposes
Black list	Entities such as programs, computers or websites that are blocked from having access to a system
Bot	A computer connected to the Internet that has been infected with malicious software, unknown to the owner, and which can therefore be controlled by someone else

Botnet	A network of bots (q.v.); using a large number of infected computers together gives their controller more power to wreak the damage they desire
Brute force attack	An attack on a computer system that involves systematically trying all possible combinations of keyboard characters until the password is found; longer passwords are obviously less susceptible to this form of attack
Bug	A small imperfection in a digital device or software that causes it to perform unexpectedly or with reduced efficiency
BYOC	Bring Your Own Cloud; the use of public cloud computing (q.v.) such as Google Docs and Dropbox to store corporate information so as to make it accessible to users when they are not able to connect to the corporate network
BYOD	Bring Your Own Device; the concept of allowing employees to use their own digital devices to access work information and perform work functions
Cloud computing	The use of a network of remote computers hosted on the Internet (as opposed to computers located in an organisation's offices) to store and process data
Cross-site scripting	See XSS
Cryptanalysis	Mathematical techniques designed to circumvent cryptographic information protection, used when the identity of the key employed in providing the protection is not known
Cryptography	The process of protecting information by turning it into a code or cypher
Data	Data is raw, unorganised symbols, facts and figures that have no meaning on their own. Data might be a list of class maths test scores. See also Information, Knowledge, Wisdom
Data breach	An event where sensitive data is disclosed to an unauthorised individual

Data integrity	Data that is complete, accurate and up to date, and has not been modified inappropriately
Data leakage	See Data breach
DDoS	See Distributed Denial of Service
Degauss	To wipe a hard disk clean of data by de-magnetising it
Denial of Service	A malicious attempt to make a website unavailable to users by interrupting the services of a computer connected to the Internet, often by bombarding it with requests from another computer so that it becomes overloaded
Digital forensics	The action of collecting, processing, analysing and archiving computer-related evidence in support of an investigation into damage of an information network
Distributed Denial of Service	A Denial of Service (q.v.) attack that uses a botnet (q.v.) to make the attack harder to combat as it is launched from many computers at the same time
DoS	See Denial of Service
Dropbox	A popular cloud computing (q.v.) service that allows people to store documents 'in the cloud' and share them with other people
Drive by pharming	Tampering with wi-fi access points so that people using them are sent to fraudulent websites rather than the ones they are expecting
Email spoofing	The forgery of an email address so that the email seems to have come from someone other than the actual sender
Exfiltration	Unauthorised transfer of data from an IT system
Exploit	A technique to breach the security of an IT system in an unauthorised fashion
Firewall	A system that prevents unauthorised access to or from a computer system; the primary method of keeping a network secure but one that is useless once intruders have breached it

Google Dork	A clever Google search query that finds loopholes in websites that allow hackers to break in and cause trouble
Google hacking	The process of using Google Dorks (q.v.)
Hacker	An individual who tries to gain unauthorised access to an information system
Information	Information is data (q.v.) that has been given some context or organisation that means it can be analysed, understood or used in some way. How well Percy scored in a maths test compared to his classmates is information. See also Data, Knowledge, Wisdom
Information security policy	A set of rules and guidelines that describes how an organisation protects and distributes corporate information
IPS	Intrusion prevention system
IP spoofing	A process where a hacker gains access to a computer system by masquerading as a trusted computer; they do this by 'spoofing' the trusted computer's identity or IP address
Jailbreaking	The process of tinkering with the operating system of Apple products including iPhones in order to free them from limitations imposed by Apple; the process allows users to install apps that are not approved by Apple; these apps can be a security risk as they can contain malware used to create 'backdoors' or download 'logic bombs' into corporate networks
Keylogging	Malware that records a keyboard user's keystroke as a way of stealing secret data such as passwords
Knowledge	Knowledge is information (q.v.) combined with other information. So for instance the sad fact that Percy's maths test score was the worst test score in 10 years is knowledge. See also Data, Information, Wisdom

Logic bomb	A program designed to be inserted into a computer so that, at a particular time or if a particular condition is satisfied (e.g. a person's network access is cancelled because they have been sacked), a set of harmful instructions (such as erasing files) will be carried out
Malicious code	Software in a computer system designed to create effects that are not desired by the owner or operator of that computer system
Malvertising	Advertising that contains malware or that direct users to a site that will upload malware to their computer
Malware	Software that damages a system or a device by performing an unauthorised process such as shutting it down or stealing information such as login details
Man in the middle	Someone who intercepts communications between one system and another; in cyber security this could be a criminal who sets up a fake wi-fi system in order to steal the login details of people who use it
Packet sniffing	See Sniffing
Patch	A piece of software designed to fix a software bug including security vulnerabilities
Pen test	See Penetration test
Penetration test	A process whereby 'friendly' assessors try to circumvent security features in order to see how they might be able to break into or damage digital systems
Pharming	The practice of directing Internet users to a fake website in order to obtain personal information such as passwords; the process involves infecting the victim's computer so that when they type in a website address like www.mybank.com they are in fact taken to a site that may look like mybank.com but is in fact controlled by criminals

Phishing	Sending mass emails that pretend to offer services or information companies in order to induce individuals to download a malicious attachment or visit a fake website where they will be asked to reveal personal information, such as passwords and credit card numbers
Ping flood attack	A Denial of Service attack that uses a large number of 'pings' (a small file sent as a query to a computer to see If It connected to another computer)
Ping of death attack	A method of making a computer crash by sending it a malformed ping file that the computer cannot handle (see ping flood attack)
Ransom-ware	An attack on a computer using software that is designed to deny access to information and processes on that computer until a ransom is paid
Rooting	The process of getting access to the operating system of an Android phone with the intention of altering it or installing unsupported apps; this process can leave mobile phones vulnerable to all sorts of malware which could in turn infect corporate networks
Rootkit	A piece of software that hides programs and processes running on a computer (e.g. keylogging software q.v.) in order to conceal computer misuse or theft
Secure socket layer	A commonly used method for securing information that is passed over the Internet
Shadow IT	Parallel informal corporate networks. See BYOC
SIEM	Security Information and Event Management; system for detecting attempted and actual intrusions into IT networks
Smishing	Phishing (q.v.) using SMS messaging
Smurf attack	A type of Denial of Service attack (q.v.)
Sniffing	Monitoring data travelling over a network; unauthorised sniffing can be used to steal data

Social engineering	An attack that doesn't rely on technology but rather exploits human behaviour and trust; phishing (q.v.) is a common social engineering attack
Spear-phishing	A phishing (q.v.) email sent to an individual or employees of a particular organisation, containing personalised and relevant information that makes the email appear more credible
Spoofing	Pretending to be something you are not. See IP spoofing and email spoofing
Spyware	Software that records your behaviour on a computer; often used by advertising companies to record which websites you have visited, it can also be used by hackers to steal sensitive information
SQL injection	The corruption of a database by the use of a database command (using the SQL computer language) that is 'injected' into the database via a form (e.g. a login form) in a website
SSL	See Secure socket layer
SYN flood attack	A type of Denial of Service attack (q.v.)
Trojan or Trojan Horse	Software that seems to have a useful function, but also has a hidden malicious function that is designed to evade security and cause damage
Virus	A computer program that can 'infect' a computer program or file (like an email) without the knowledge of the user and then spread to other computers as the program or file is shared
VPN	Virtual private network. (1) Ability for a computer to connect with an office network via the Internet; (2) Commercial service designed to protect wi-fi users by acting as a barrier between the data they access and the wi-fi provider
Watering hole attack	An attack aimed at a group of individuals. For instance the attacker might identify a website that members of a group commonly use and then infect it in the hope of subsequently infecting a member of that group

White list	A limited set of entities such as programs, computers or websites that are allowed to have access to a system
Wisdom	Wisdom is knowledge (q.v.) combined with experience. If Percy understands that he needs to work harder in his maths class next week if he wants to avoid being held back after school again, then he is showing wisdom. See also Data, Information, Knowledge
Worm	A malicious program that can use computer networks to spread itself without the need for any action by the computer user
XSS	Cross-site scripting, a technique of infecting a user's computer via a trusted website into which malicious code is injected through a web form like a login form
Zero day attack	An attack that exploits a previously unknown flaw in the security of a computer system; because it is unknown (except perhaps to criminals around the world), no one has had any time to fix the flaw, hence 'zero day'

Index

Printed in the United States
by Baker & Taylor Publisher Services